The MAILBOX®
The Education Center®

grade
Preschool

Learning Centers

D1476102

THE BEST OF
The MAILBOX®
MAGAZINE

Our best learning center ideas
from the 1995–2004 issues of
The Mailbox® magazine

- **Literacy**
- **Math**
- **Science**
- **Sensory**
- **Water and Sand**
- **Fine Motor and Gross Motor**
- **Art**
- **Blocks**
- **Dramatic Play**
- **Games and Puzzles**

Editorial Team: Becky S. Andrews, Kimberley Bruck, Karen P. Shelton, Diane Badden, Thad H. McLaurin, Sharon Murphy, Karen A. Brudnak, Hope Rodgers, Dorothy C. McKinney

Production Team: Lori Z. Henry, Pam Crane, Rebecca Saunders, Jennifer Tipton Cappoen, Chris Curry, Sarah Foreman, Theresa Lewis Goode, Greg D. Rieves, Barry Slate, Donna K. Teal, Zane Williard, Tazmen Carlisle, Marsha Heim, Lynette Dickerson, Mark Rainey

Includes Colorful
Ready-to-Go Pieces

www.themailbox.com

©2006 The Mailbox®
All rights reserved.
ISBN10 #1-56234-720-9 • ISBN13 #978-156234-720-8

Manufactured in the United States
10 9 8 7 6 5 4 3 2 1

Table of Contents

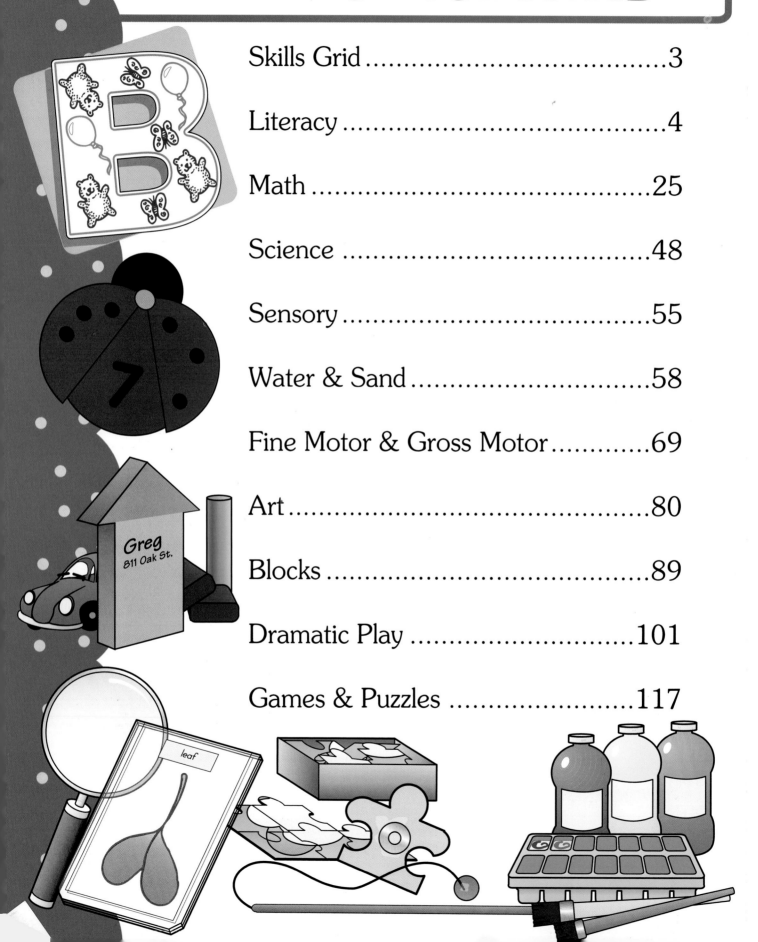

Skills Grid

	Literacy	Math	Science	Sensory	Water & Sand	Fine Motor & Gross Motor	Art	Blocks	Dramatic Play	Games & Puzzles
Literacy Skills										
letter recognition	4									
sound of the letter *P*	4									
letter formation	5									
letter sounds	5, 6									
letters	6									
names: matching letters	7									
print awareness	7, 17									
spelling names	8, 9									
color words	8									
matching uppercase letters	9									
matching uppercase and lowercase letters	9			61						
storytelling	12								92	
listening	13									
writing letters	14, 15, 16									
writing names	15									
writing letters and words	16, 17									
Math Skills										
counting		25, 26, 27, 28, 29, 30		56, 57		71, 73, 75				
one-to-one correspondence				57		57, 75				
numeral recognition		25, 26, 29			60			89		
numeral matching		26								
number identification		27, 28								
number matching		29								
sequencing numbers				61						
patterning		30, 31								
match by size		32								
sort by color		32, 33	57							
match by color		33,	57	63						
sorting		34								118
sorting and counting		35							103	
match by shape		35								
visual discrimination										117, 118, 119, 120
problem solving										118
spatial sense										121
Science Skills										
observation: birds			48							
observation: water pollution			49							
observation: ice				62						
magnets			48, 51							
space			49							
observation: a variety of materials			50							
rain forest			50							
simulating a dinosaur dig					64					
simulating an archeological dig					66					
simulating space travel									108	
simulating undersea exploration									109	
simulating an animal burrow									110	
dental health			51	56						
using a magnifying glass			52							
mixing colors			52	62			85, 86			
Fine-Motor and Gross-Motor Skills										
cutting						69, 70			101	
lacing						69, 70				
tearing						70				
play dough						70, 72, 73, 74, 75				
rolling a ball						71				117
tossing						71				

Needles in a Haystack

Hide some craft sticks (needles) in some crinkle paper (hay) and send your students on a **letter** hunt! To make a needle, write a letter your youngsters may recognize, such as the first letter from a child's name, on one end of a wooden craft stick. Then make another needle with a matching letter. When you have several pairs of letter needles prepared, put them into a sensory tub filled with yellow or tan crinkle paper (or another hay substitute). Each child can look for needles in the haystack, trying to find pairs of matching letters.

Christin Maschio
I'm Special Learning Center Inc.
Yalesville, CT

Pick a Patch of *P* s

Get the dirt on this unique sensory experience that reinforces the **sound of the letter *P*.** Laminate and cut out the seed picture cards on page 19. Put the seeds in a tub filled with soil or sand. Add a pair of gloves, a plastic shovel, and a pumpkin pail to the area. Invite a child visiting the center to use the shovel to find the programmed seeds and put them in the pumpkin pail. To reinforce his learning, sing the song below with him, substituting the word *pumpkin* with the items on the seeds.

(adapt to the tune of "The Farmer in the Dell")

[Pumpkin] begins with *P*.
[Pumpkin] begins with *P*.
/p/ /p/ /p/ /p/ /p/ /p/
[Pumpkin] begins with *P*.

adapted from an idea by Henry Fergus
Phoenix, AZ

Letter Learning

Help your students practice **letter formation** and sounds with this simple activity. In advance, use a pencil to make a large outline of a letter on each of several sheets of white copy paper. Provide small incentive stickers or rubber stamps that show pictures of items beginning with that letter. Encourage a child to place the stickers along the outline of the letter or to stamp the image repeatedly along the outline.

As a variation, provide two different stickers or stamps, and challenge a child to use both images to create an *ABAB* pattern along the letter's outline.

J. Gaye Drummond
Redeemer Lutheran Preschool and School
Tucson, AZ

Driving Sounds

If your preschoolers are crazy for cars, they'll love this center! Use colorful masking tape to form a large **letter** on the floor. Provide small toy cars and invite youngsters to drive them over the lines and curves of the letter. When students are behind the wheel, encourage them to make the sound of the letter they are cruising. It's time to go for a drive!

Amy Aloi
Bollman Bridge RECC
Jessup, MD

Stamps and Sounds

Do your preschoolers love rubber stamps? Then they'll love this stamping activity that reinforces **letter sounds!** As you study each letter of the alphabet, place large outlines of the letter in your literacy area, along with one or more rubber stamps of items beginning with that letter. Invite a child at this center to stamp the images within the outline of the letter. *B* is for butterflies, bears, and balloons!

Shelley Williams
Children's College
Layton, UT

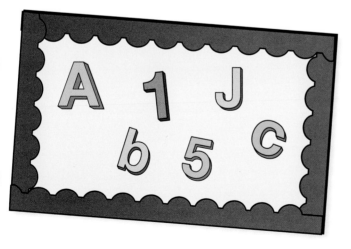

M Is for Magnetic

Make this a **letter and number** center that youngsters are sure to be attracted to! Obtain a piece of sheet metal from a home supply store and nail it to a wall. Then cover the sheet with bulletin board paper and add border if desired. Arrange magnetic letters and numerals on the board.

Michelle West
Denton City County Day School, Denton, TX

Alphabet Boards

These personalized workmats and plastic **letters** spell out fun at your literacy center. Personalize a sheet of construction paper to make a work mat for each child. Gather enough plastic letters so that each child has the letters needed to spell her name. Store each child's set of letters in a separate, labeled resealable plastic bag. Put the workmats and bags at a center. At the center, a child chooses a workmat and the corresponding set of letters. She then matches the letters to the letters on the mat to spell her name or a class-mate's name.

Bonnie McKenzie
Cheshire Country Day School, Cheshire, CT

Milk Cap Names

Use the caps from milk jugs to offer your little ones a serving of **print awareness**! Personalize a zippered bag for each child. Then write the letters of each child's name on individual milk caps and store the caps inside the corresponding zippered bag. Place children's bags at your literacy center. A child finds her bag and removes the milk caps from it. Then she uses the bag label as a guide as she arranges the lettered milk caps to spell her name. Impressive!

Lisa Terry
First United Methodist Daycare
Muscle Shoals, AL

Literacy

Name Tubes

Help your preschoolers spell their **names** with this idea that's totally tubular! To prepare, cut a number of paper towel tubes into one-inch sections. Label each tube section with one letter from a child's name until you've spelled every child's name. Place each child's tube pieces in a separate zippered plastic bag labeled with her picture. Have a child remove the tube pieces from her bag and line them up on a tabletop to spell her name.

When you're finished with this center, invite youngsters to glue their tube pieces together side by side to make a permanent name sculpture to take home!

Mary Patton
Washington School, Rushville, IL

Dip Into Color Matching

Invite students to don painters' caps and dip into this center for some **color-matching** fun! To prepare, cut out eight bucket shapes from gray felt. Using the eight basic colors, cut paint-drip shapes from felt (see the illustration). Then hot-glue each shape onto a different bucket. Glue on felt letters or use fabric paint to label each bucket with the appropriate color word. To make a handle for each bucket, gently push the ends of a pipe cleaner through the sides of a bucket, and then twist the wire to hold it in place. Hot-glue or sew each prepared bucket onto a cloth background, leaving the top open to form a pocket. For each bucket, program a paint stick with the corresponding color word and paint the end of the stick with the matching color.

To use this center, encourage a child to place each paint stick in the matching bucket. Challenge older preschoolers to use the color words to match each pair. No spills or splatters here—just good, clean, color-matching fun!

Terry Steinke
Emmaus Lutheran School, Indianapolis, IN

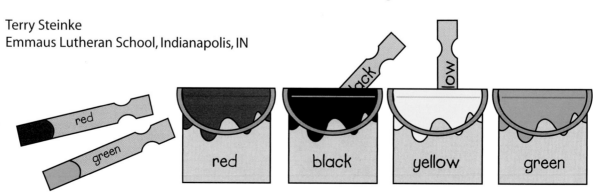

Pick a Letter

When a child spells his **name**, he wins this small-group or partner game! Place student name strips and a container of letter tiles at a table. First, each player finds his name strip. Then the students take turns drawing single tiles from the container. If the letter a child draws is in his name, he lays it on his name strip. If it is not, he may give the letter to another player who can use it, or he puts the letter back in the container. The first player to spell his name wins!

Shelley Hoster
Jack and Jill Early Learning Center
Norcross, GA

"Alpha-Cookies"

Cook up some fun with this tasty **alphabet-matching** game! To begin, cut out 26 craft foam cookies. Hot-glue a different foam uppercase letter (or write one with a permanent marker) on each cookie. Store your cookies in a cookie tin labeled " 'Alpha-Cookies.' " Tape paper uppercase letters to a cookie sheet; then cover the sheet with clear Con-Tact covering. To use the items, a child uses a spatula to slide each cookie onto its matching cookie sheet letter.

As a variation, program a second set of cookies with lowercase letters. Have a child similarly match the cookies to the uppercase letters on the pan.

Donna Allen
A-Is-For-Apple Preschool
Glen Dale, WV

9

Literacy

Bedtime Stories for Baby Dolls

Invite your little ones to pitter-patter to your **reading area** for bedtime stories. Place several dolls, small rocking chairs, doll beds, and baby blankets in the area. Next add plenty of board books that your students can "read," such as nursery rhyme books. Encourage your youngsters to visit the area to read bedtime stories to the dolls.

Laura Bentley
Captain John Palliser Elementary
Calgary, Alberta, Canada

A Reading Pond

Create a setting in your **reading area** that your youngsters will dive into—a reading pond! To make a reading pond, place a round blue tablecloth on the floor of a wading pool to resemble water. Randomly place round green pillows in the pond to represent lily pads. Also place turtle and fish puppets in and around the pond. Position live or artificial plants around the pond area. On a table near the pond, provide books about pond life, plus frog headbands or hats. To use this center, allow two children at a time to don frog hats, choose books from the table, and enjoy reading in the reading pond. No doubt this center will make a splash!

Kate Taluga
Big Bend Community Coordinated
  Child Care
Tallahassee, FL

A Cool Pool

Swim into summer reading with a child's wading pool placed in your **reading area**. Since you don't want your books or your young readers getting wet in this center, invite your youngsters to make some imaginary water by sitting inside the pool and cutting blue crepe paper streamers and construction paper scraps into small pieces. After the cutting practice, remove the scissors and add some small inflatable swim rings and perhaps a fish-shaped pillow or two. Now your pool is all set for diving into a good book!

Jill Simon
Discovery Place YWCA
Poland, OH

Camp Out With a Good Book

You're sure to have a group of happy campers in your **reading area** when you transform it into a campsite! Set up a small pop-up tent; then add a couple of cozy sleeping bags, some pillows, and a big cooler filled with books. Make the area even more fun by including a backpack filled with story tapes and a tape player with earphones. After setting up this camping area, don't be surprised if your little ones have a craving for roasted marshmallows at snacktime!

Lisa Leonardi
Norfolk, MA

Reading's a Picnic!

Time to grab a picnic basket and some good books for your **reading area!** Bring the outdoors in by spreading a picnic blanket on the floor, tucking some books about spring into a picnic basket, and tossing in a few pairs of sunglasses. Then invite youngsters to settle in for some spring reading. Just leave the ants outside!

Lisa Leonardi
Norfolk, MA

Clever Clings

Use window clings to help your little ones develop their **storytelling** skills! Slide a blank sheet of paper into each of five or six plastic sheet protectors. Store the pages in a one-inch binder. Then choose window clings with a related theme—such as flowers, letters, animals, or favorite characters—and stick them to the protectors. Encourage youngsters to peel off the clings and reposition them to tell a story.

Carole Watkins
Holy Family Child Care Center
Crown Point, IN

Five Little Ducks

A few fun props will get your preschoolers waddling on over to your **listening** area! Provide a tape of the traditional song "Five Little Ducks." Purchase some rubber duckies—five small ones and one larger one to be the mama. Add a large blue plastic bowl to the area too. Then invite a child to listen to and act out the song using the toy ducks and the blue bowl pond.

Cathy Consford
Buda Primary Early Learning Center
Buda, TX

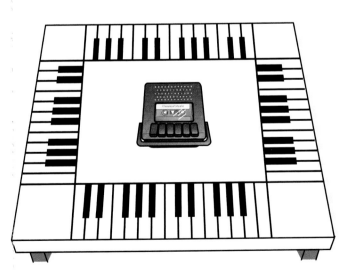

Ticklin' the Ivories

At this **listening** center, youngsters get in tune with their musical talents by playing a pretend piano. Use masking tape to secure a sheet of white bulletin board paper to a tabletop. Next, make four copies of the piano keyboard pattern on page 18 and cut them out. Tape each pattern around the table as shown. Put an audiotape of piano music in a cordless tape recorder; then place it in the center of the table. As the music plays, invite your students to pretend to play the piano. Soon your room will be full of baby Beethovens!

Patricia Moeser
U. W. Preschool Lab Site 1
Madison, WI

Cinnamon Letters

This activity for your **writing** center will smell as good as it looks! Supply youngsters with cinnamon sticks and sheets of sandpaper cut into the shapes of various letters. Have little ones trace the lines and curves of the sandpaper letters with the cinnamon sticks. Once your preschoolers get the hang of writing with the cinnamon sticks, provide uncut sheets of sandpaper and invite them to write letters (or make drawings) freehand.

Karen M. Pyne
Tower Hill School
Randolph, MA

Rub 'em and Write 'Em

"Look! Letters!" That's what your students will be saying when they try this crayon-rubbing activity. Use double-sided tape to stick die-cut letters to the top of your **writing** table. Then spread a piece of white bulletin board paper over the tabletop and tape the edges in place. Provide peeled crayons; then invite little ones to rub the sides of the crayons over the paper and reveal the letters. Encourage them to practice forming the letters on the paper near the rubbings. For added learning fun, have more advanced students draw things that begin with that letter.

Sweet Writing

Fill your classroom with the sweet scent of chocolate, and little ones will instantly be inspired to **write!** Mix up a batch of chocolate pudding. Then give each child at the center a piece of waxed paper and a spoonful of pudding. Encourage him to spread the pudding over the waxed paper and use his finger to write letters, numbers, or his name. To erase, he simply spreads the pudding again. Mmm! This writing activity is truly finger-lickin' good!

Brenda Horn
Livingston Elementary, Livingston, IL

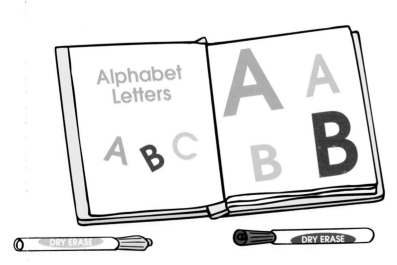

Write 'n' Wipe

Your little ones will make memories as they use this photo album idea to practice their **writing** skills. Fill the pages of an album that has plastic page protectors with letter-shaped and geometric cutouts. Also fill the pages with cards labeled with students' names. Place the album in your literacy center along with dry erase markers and tissues. (Slim dry erase markers are less pungent.) Encourage your little ones to write, wipe, and then write again!

Jenny Unruh
Georgia Matthews Elementary
Garden City, KS

Literacy

Ready, Set, Write!

At this writing center, young-sters **write letters** found in their classmates' names. Label a photo of each child with his name. Laminate the photos for use at a writing center. Put the pictures at the center along with various writing tools and paper. Encourage children at the center to find each other's pictures, identify their names, and practice writing letters in each other's names. Ready, set, write!

Adina Castillo
Alain Locke Charter Academy
Chicago, IL

Magic Paper

If you have preschoolers interested in **writing letters and words,** encourage them to use some magic paper—an over-head transparency! Write a simple word or a child's name on a sheet of white paper. Place the magic paper (the transparency) over the white paper. Give the child dry-erase markers and encourage her to trace the letters. Remove the magic paper and enjoy her look of delight as she sees she's written the word all by herself! An old sock slipped over the child's hand makes an excellent eraser, so she can reuse the marvelous magic paper to write another word!

Missy Glunt
Child Advocates of Blair County CIRS
Roaring Spring, PA

The "Write" Time

Stock your center with various types of supplies that can be used for **print** exploration and writing, such as colored pencils, markers, alphabet stamps, magnet letters and a magnetboard, felt letters and a felt board, and various sizes and colors of papers. Cut out the picture cards on page 21 and place them at the center. Consider also preparing a reference book with a page for each child, displaying her name and photo. For young learners, this open-ended center is "write" on track!

Donna Leonard
Head Start
Dyersville, IA

Copy Kids

You can count on little ones being eager to **copy words**. For an easy-to-manage fine-motor activity, attach the hook sides of six Velcro dots to a poster board chart. Cut out the picture cards on page 23. Press the loop side of a Velcro dot on the back of each card and then display the cards on the chart. Place the chart within your youngsters' reach. A child removes the card he wants. He copies the word on provided paper and draws his own picture clue. Then he returns the card to the chart.

Donna Leonard
Head Start
Dyersville, IA

Piano Keyboard Pattern

Use with "Ticklin' the Ivories" on page 13.

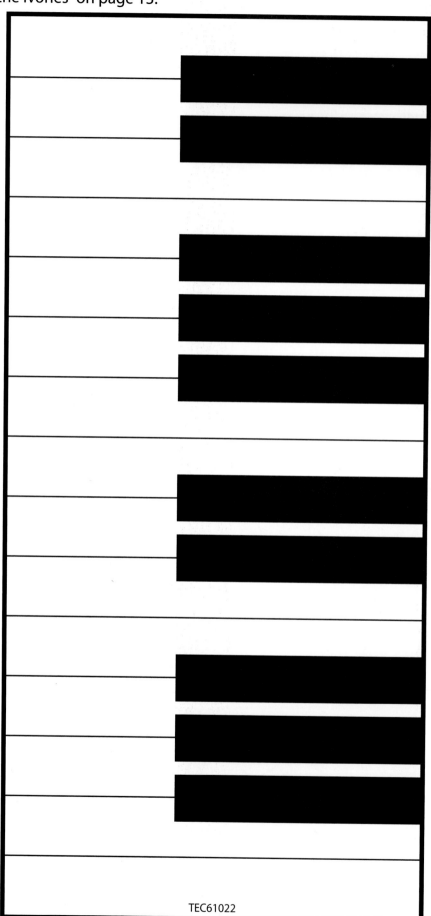

TEC61022

TEC61022

TEC61022

TEC61022

TEC61022

TEC61022

TEC61022

TEC61022

TEC61022

dog

hat

pan

car

bed

pig

TEC61022

TEC61022

TEC61022

TEC61022

TEC61022

TEC61022

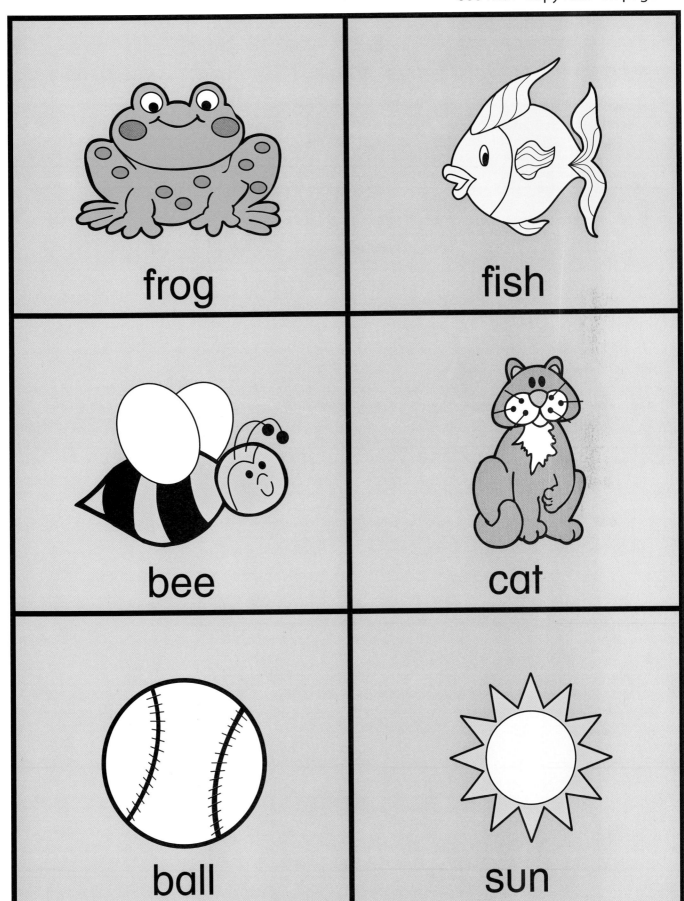

frog

fish

bee

cat

ball

sun

24

Monster Footprints

Make a supply of wacky footprints for some monstrous **counting** fun. From black construction paper, cut monster footprints in odd shapes and with varying numbers of toes. Laminate the footprints for durability. Invite little ones to count the toes on each footprint, sort or match the footprints by shape, or create a trail with a specific number of footprints. Hey—monster feet are neat!

Annette Hulen
Glendale, AZ

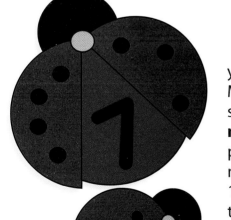

Ladybug Counting

Little ones will spread their wings and fly over to your math area for some number fun with ladybugs! Make a set of ladybug manipulatives to help your students practice **counting and numeral recognition.** To make one ladybug, cut out a construction paper copy of the pattern on page 36. Use a permanent marker to label the ladybug with a numeral from 1 to 10; then draw the corresponding number of dots on the wing set. Fasten the patterns together with a brad as shown. Invite a child at this center to count the dots on a ladybug's wings and then spread the wings to see the corresponding numeral.

Kathy Myles, Hicksville Nursery School, Hicksville, NY

Math

Bubble Count

Something's fishy about this math center idea. It's how much fun youngsters have practicing **counting and numeral recognition!** To prepare the game, cut out the fish cards on pages 37 and 39. Arrange the fish on a piece of poster board; then trace around them. Use glitter glue to make a different number of bubbles from one to ten above each fish outline. Remove the fish. To use the game, a child counts the number of bubbles above a fish outline. Then he puts the fish with the corresponding numeral on the board beneath the bubbles.

Trish Draper
Millarville Community School
Millarville, Alberta, Canada

Match the Hearts

Youngsters will love this **numeral-matching** center. From an old deck of playing cards, remove the numbered cards in the heart suit. Cut each card in half crosswise so that its number shows on both halves. Put the cut cards at your math center, and encourage a child to match the halves of each card.

Jennifer Barton, Elizabeth Green School, Newington, CT

A Little Book of Numbers

Combine **number identification, counting, and fine-motor skills** with this center idea! To prepare, program a booklet page for each numeral from 1 to 10. Add number words if desired. Then copy each page on different colored paper to make a class supply. As you introduce each number, put copies of the corresponding booklet page in your math center, along with a hole puncher. Each child punches a matching number of holes in a page. Compile each child's pages into a minibooklet with a cover that reads "My Little Book of Numbers." Then send the booklets home for youngsters to read and touch!

Sarah Booth
Messiah Nursery School
South Williamsport, PA

How Many Scoops?

Dish up some **counting** fun with the help of some pretend ice cream! To prepare, write a different numeral from 1 to 10 in the bottom of each of ten foam bowls. Put the bowls in your math center, along with an ice-cream scoop and some play-dough balls in a variety of cool and creamy ice-cream colors! Invite a pair of children to visit the center. Have one child choose a bowl and put in the corresponding number of play-dough ice-cream scoops. Have him serve it to his partner, who pretends to eat the ice cream while counting to check the server's work. Then have the children switch roles and dish up more fun!

Shelley Banzhaf
Maywood, NE

27

Math

How Many Chicks?

One peep at this activity and a little one's **number identification and counting** skills are reinforced! Label a large plastic egg for each numeral from 1 to 10. Inside each egg, put a corresponding number of pom-poms to serve as baby chicks. Then put the eggs in a basket at your math center. A child chooses an egg, identifies the numeral on it, and then opens the egg and counts the chicks inside. When he's verified that the set of chicks matches the numeral on the egg, he counts the chicks again as he returns them to the egg. Then he snaps the egg shut. Time to count some more chickens before they hatch!

Lynda Williamson
Grandlake High School
Lake Charles, LA

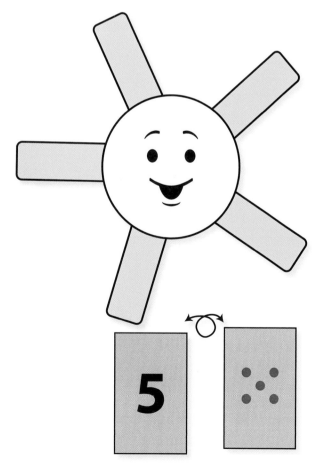

Sunrays

You can **count** on lots of sunshine at this time of year—even inside your classroom! Cut a large circle and ten long rectangles from yellow poster board. Cut out the cards on page 41. Place the paper sun, the sunrays, and the number cards at your math center. Invite a child to choose a card, count out the corresponding number of rays to place around the sun, and then flip the card to double-check his counting.

adapted from an idea by
Kimberly A. Dawes
Little Blessings Daycare
Portsmouth, NH

Abracadabra!

It won't take much hocus-pocus to entice students to practice **numeral-recognition and counting** skills at this center! Make one copy of the spinner and three copies of the bunny cards on page 43. Also make two copies of the gameboard on page 44. Cut out the spinner and mount it on top of a plastic top hat (available at party stores). Program the bunny cards from 1–7, to make two sets of game cards, and cut them out. Store each set of cards in a separate resealable plastic bag and place the bags at the center with the gameboards.

To play, each child at the center takes a gameboard and a set of bunnies. In turn, each child spins the spinner, then puts the bunny with the matching numeral on his gameboard. Play continues until each child's gameboard is covered with bunnies. Pulling rabbits from a hat for numeral-recognition practice works like magic every time!

Debra L. Erickson
Milan-Dummer Area Kindergarten
Milan, NH

Telephone Booth

Create an imaginary telephone booth to help youngsters practice **number-matching skills**—and memorize their phone numbers too! Simply cut a tall doorway from one side of a donated refrigerator box. Cover the outside of the box with paint or paper. Then encourage little ones to paint numerals all over the outside of the booth. Then, for each child, prepare a sentence strip programmed with both her name and her phone number. Store the strips inside the booth. Add a chair, a phone book, a toy or real phone (minus the cord), and some plastic numerals or sturdy numeral cutouts. Invite each youngster to match the manipulative numerals to the phone-number strips before dialing her own and her classmates' numbers.

adapted from an idea by Christine M. Zieleniewski
St. Cecilia School
Kearny, NJ

Math

Fine-Feathered Counting

We're not talking turkey! This game helps your preschoolers **count** and play a partner game. To make a gameboard, glue a construction paper copy of the pattern on page 45 onto tagboard to make a turkey without feathers. (Leave the top of the turkey body unglued so the feathers can slide in.) Make a second gameboard. Also cut out at least 12 construction paper feathers. To play, one child in a pair rolls a large die and then puts that number of feathers on his turkey gameboard. The partners take turns in this manner until there are no feathers left. How many feathers does your turkey have?

Melisa Jennings
Charlie Brown Nursery School
Pulaski, NY

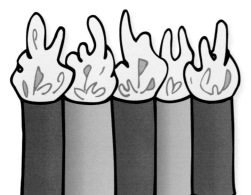

Festive Candle Patterning

Add these festive candles to youngsters' **patterning** play. To make one candle, glue tissue paper around a toilet paper tube. Crumple a sheet of yellow tissue paper to resemble a flame; then glue the bottom of the flame inside one end of the tube. Make a supply of candles in two different colors; then place the candles in a basket at the center. Invite each child to arrange the candles in a pattern. As you admire your little one's candle arrangement, ask her to describe the attribute she used for patterning. You're sure to hear cheerful chants of "red candle, green candle, red candle…"

Michelle Rogers
Ft. Dodge Cooperative Preschool
Ft. Dodge, IA

Sunshine Patterning

Here's a hot idea for helping youngsters understand sizes and simple **patterns!** Tape a large yellow construction paper circle onto a tabletop to represent the sun. Cut a supply of rectangles from yellow construction paper in two lengths. To use the center, a child arranges the rays around the circle in an alternating pattern of long and short.

Kimberly Curry
Cunningham Creek Elementary
Jacksonville, FL

Valentine Chain

This heart-to-heart paper chain will help your preschoolers with **patterning!** To prepare, cut a large supply of 1" x 12" strips from valentine colors of construction paper. Fold each strip in half. At your math center, demonstrate how to fold the two ends of each strip together to make a heart shape (see illustration); then glue the ends together with a glue stick. Have each child make a heart from a strip of her choice. Then have her choose a different color. Have her thread the strip into the heart she's made before folding and gluing it into another heart shape. Have her then make a third heart using her original color. Have her continue following the two-color pattern to make a chain of the desired length. When every child has made a pattern chain, connect them all together and display the chain of hearts on your classroom ceiling or wall.

Shelly Post, Helping Hands Preschool, Great Bend, KS

Math

Tops and Bottoms

Focus on **size matching** with a center that makes good use of gift boxes and wrapping paper. Collect gift boxes in assorted sizes. For a challenge, include a few that are the same size. Wrap the tops and bottoms of the boxes in wrapping paper, but don't make the tops and bottoms match. Ask students at this center to find the right top for each box bottom by paying attention to size, not the patterns on the papers.

Sharon Jefferies and Susan Tornebene
Palma Sola Elementary
Bradenton, FL

All Sorts of Fun

Use colored tape to divide a round or square table into a sorting area with two, three, or four sections. To encourage students to **sort by color,** tape a different-colored shape in each section if desired. Keep a variety of manipulatives nearby so that individual students or groups of students can come to the table for plenty of sorting fun.

Kim Hilario
Adobe Christian Preschool
Petaluma, CA

32

Colorful Collections

A rainbow of colorful collections awaits your youngsters with this **sorting** game. Collect various colors of baby-wipe containers. Write the corresponding color word on each container. Gather a variety of small items that are the same colors as the containers; then place the items in a basket. Place the color containers and the basket in a center. To use the center, a child sorts the items by color into the containers.

Michelle West
Denton City County Day School
Denton, TX

Hearts and Arrows

Send your little cupids on a **color-matching** spree! To prepare, cut a supply of small hearts from various colors of construction paper. Using markers in matching colors, program a corresponding number of spring-type clothespins with arrows. If desired, also use the markers to draw designs on the hearts; then laminate the hearts for durability. Have a child at this center clip each clothespin to the heart of the matching color.

LeeAnn Collins
Sunshine House Preschool
Lansing, MI

Math

Doughnut Sorting

To prepare for this sweet **sorting** center, visit a local bakery or doughnut shop and request donations of unused doughnut boxes. Cut a supply of doughnut shapes from craft foam. Next, create different sets of doughnuts by gluing craft-foam frosting or other craft items onto the shapes. Place the doughnuts in a container or on a tray and invite students to sort each set of doughnuts into a different box. One dozen chocolate doughnuts, please!

adapted from an idea by Karen Reed
Trailside Daycare, Providence, RI

Load 'em Up!

Sort 'em out, then load 'em up! Your little ones will become **sorting** experts when you convert your math center into a train station. In advance, collect several brightly colored, empty disposable baby-wipe containers. Next, duplicate the train engine pattern on page 46. Color the engine, laminate it, and then cut it out. Hot-glue the engine to the side of a wipe container. Then use small pieces of Velcro fasteners to connect the containers, creating a train. Place the train at your center along with a large bin containing items such as Lincoln Logs and toy cars. Invite youngsters to sort the items and then load them into the train cars. Choo-choo! The sorting train is coming through!

Joan Frenzel and Donna Catli
Rochester, NY

Yikes! Spikes!

Sorting and counting are "dino-mite" at this math center! Purchase a bag of colorful plastic clothespins. Then, for each color of clothespin, make one copy of the stegosaurus pattern from page 47 on the corresponding color of construction paper. Label each pattern with its color word. Next, laminate the patterns for durability and cut them out. Place the patterns and clothespins at your math center. A child chooses a stegosaurus and clips the same color of clothespins to its back for spikes. When he's added as many spikes as he likes, he counts them. Yikes! That's a lot of spikes!

Kimberly Curry
Cunningham Creek Elementary
Jacksonville, FL

It's Shape Time!

Looking for shape fun? If so, then try this concentration game to help youngsters learn **shapes.** Gather an even number of classroom photos. Cut pairs of photos into matching geometric shapes. Glue the shapes onto separate cards. To play a game of concentration, a child spreads the cards facedown on the floor. She then flips two cards. If photos of matching shapes are found, the child keeps the cards. If no match is found, she turns the cards facedown again. She continues until all of the matches have been found. This idea's a match for shape recognition!

Maureen F. Guepin
Lowell, MA

35

Ladybug Pattern
Use with "Ladybug Counting" on page 25.

TEC61022

TEC61022

TEC61022

TEC61022

TEC61022

TEC61022

5	10
4	9
3	8
2	7
1	6

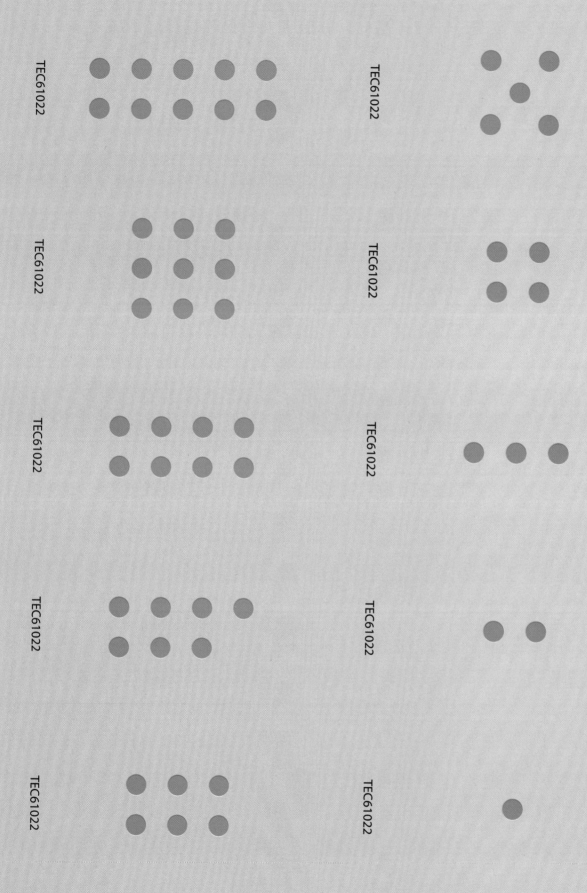

TEC61022

TEC61022

TEC61022

TEC61022

TEC61022

TEC61022

TEC61022

TEC61022

TEC61022

TEC61022

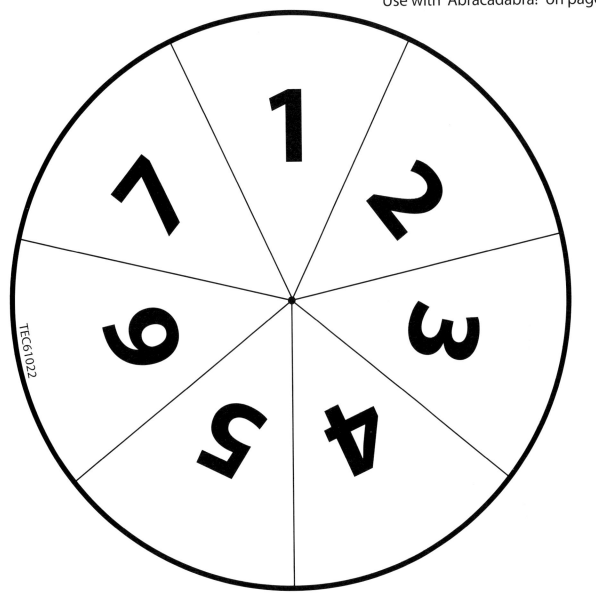

TEC61022

TEC61022   TEC61022   TEC61022   TEC61022   TEC61022

Abracadabra!

44

Note to the teacher: Use with "Abracadabra!" on page 29.

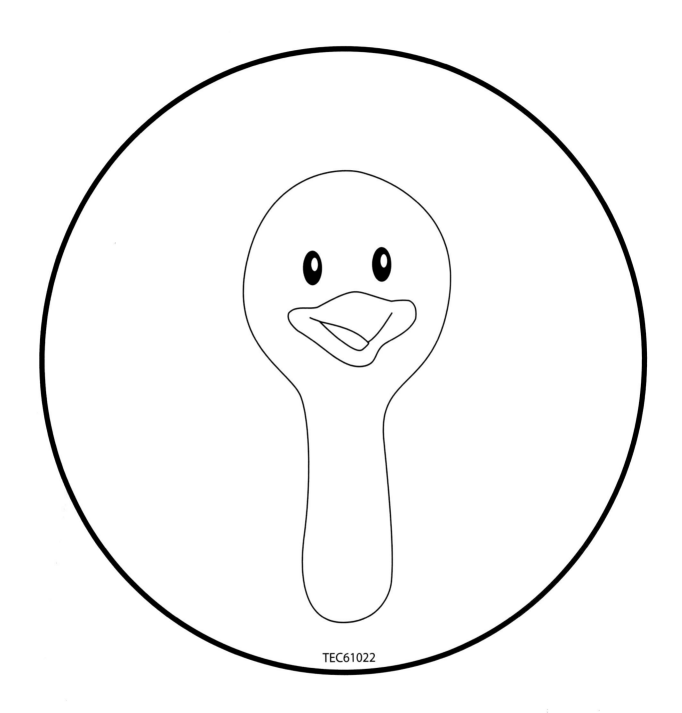

TEC61022

Train Engine Pattern

Use with "Load 'em Up!" on page 34.

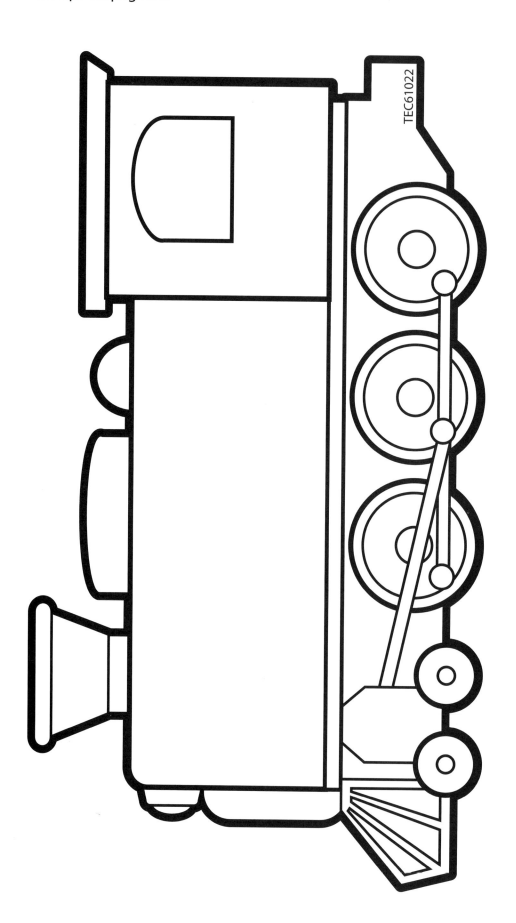

TEC61022

TEC61022

Bird-Watching

Add something special to your science center by placing a birdhouse outside the window for **observation**. Purchase an inexpensive birdhouse, or ask a parent to donate one. When a fine-feathered friend moves in, your preschoolers will be able to watch their new "pet" going about its daily routine. Encourage little ones to share their observations in a class journal. There may be even more "eggs-citement" when spring arrives!

Doris Peiffer
Head Start
Anamosa, IA

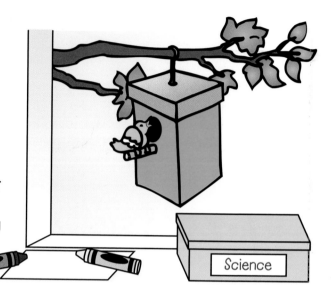

Paper Clips in a Bottle

Youngsters are sure to be attracted to this **magnetic** idea! Remove the label from a small clean soda bottle and then partially fill the bottle with play sand. Add a handful of paper clips and then hot-glue the lid on. Tie one end of a length of string to a magnetic wand and tie the other end around the neck of the bottle. A child can now explore the attraction between the magnet and the paper clips with the clips safely inside the bottle. For more magnet fun, seal paper clips and paper confetti or paper clips and rice inside a second bottle!

Cathy Consford
Buda Primary Early Learning Center
Buda, TX

Pollution Jar

This fascinating science experiment focuses on **water pollution**. Partially fill a large, clear, plastic jar with water. After discussing water pollution, have each child place a small piece of trash—such as a fast-food napkin, candy wrapper, or Popsicle stick—into the jar. Screw the lid on tightly and then secure it with duct tape. Set the jar in your science center for youngsters to observe. Ask what they think will happen to the water and to the trash. Then watch as the garbage breaks down over time and turns the clear water into a thick, brown liquid. Yuck!

Andrea Ludtke
Burnsville, MN

See the Stars

Create a petite **planetarium** for your young stargazers! Affix a variety of glow-in-the-dark stickers shaped like stars, moons, and planets to sheets of dark construction paper. Tape the paper to the underside of a table; then cover the table with a dark sheet. Add a few books about space and a couple of flashlights. Then invite your preschoolers to take turns under the table, lying back to look up at the stars and using the flashlights to read all about them!

Rhonda Hixson
St. Christopher's Center for Children
Vandalia, OH

Science

Pick-a-Pocket

Spark youngsters' curiosity at this science center that promotes **observation** skills. Hang a shoe organizer with clear pockets near your science table. Fill the pockets with materials to investigate, such as feathers, seashells, pinecones, rocks, twigs, and leaves. Also place magnifying glasses in several pockets. Now observation and exploration materials are clearly visible, and cleanup is a breeze!

Jodi Sykes
North Grade
Lake Worth, FL

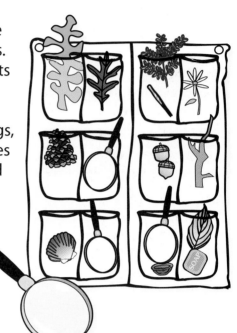

Rain Forest

Little ones will think they are actually in the Amazon when you transform an area of your room into a tropical rain forest. To create a **rain-forest** canopy, drape a large piece of camouflage net (the kind used for hunting) over any furniture in the area. Randomly place plastic or rubber snakes, frogs, crocodiles, and lizards in the netting and around the center. Also place artificial trees, vines, and plants in the center. Play a recording of rain-forest sounds (available from nature stores). What a great addition to your rain forest unit!

Glenda C. Roddey
An Academe For Children, Inc.
Springdale, AR

Terrific Teeth

Help youngsters brush up on an important **dental health** habit with this "scrub-ulous" idea. If necessary, remove the bottom covers from several empty one- or two-liter plastic bottles. Cut off the bottoms of the bottles that resemble tooth surfaces. Tape the cut edges to protect your little ones from scratches. Place the plastic teeth, several toothbrushes, and a bowl of shaving cream in a center that is located near a sink. Invite children who visit the area to practice their brushing skills on the plastic teeth. When each child is finished, have her rinse her plastic tooth and toothbrush in the sink so that another budding brusher can polish her cleaning skills. This sparkling idea is sure to get lots of toothy grins!

Crystal Sirmans
Child Care Contacts R & R
Milledgeville, GA

Start Your Engines

Your children will zoom over to this **discovery** area. Make a magnetic raceway by drawing and coloring a racetrack on a large piece of tagboard. Then cut out the cars from page 53. Laminate the track and the cars. Slide a large paper clip onto each car. Tape the ends of the tagboard raceway to the edges of two tables so that the track is suspended in air. Place the cars on the track. Invite a child to use the raceway by moving a magnet underneath the tagboard. On your mark, get set, go!

Kim Richman
The Learning Zone
Des Moines, IA

Science

Look What I See!

Encourage hands-on learning and lots of **discovery** opportunities by using these creative science slides. Obtain a number of the thin plastic covers used for baseball trading cards. Insert a different item into each slide. For example, you might include a leaf, a piece of material that has an interesting texture, a cotton ball, and a dried flower. Label each slide by its contents. Place these slides in your discovery center along with several magnifying lenses. Have children visiting this center use the magnifying lenses to carefully examine the slides and discuss what they see. No messy cleanup here—just up-close and personal learning!

Clara White
Western School
N. Lauderdale, FL

Color Mixing

Mesmerize your little ones with these **discovery** bottles that change colors! To make one, fill a clear plastic bottle with equal parts of colored water and colored lamp oil. Be sure the colors of the water and the oil are different primary colors that will blend into a new color. For example, use blue oil and yellow water. Next, hot-glue the lid onto the bottle. Make several discovery bottles with different colors and set them at the center. Invite each child to choose a bottle and identify the two different colors. Then direct him to vigorously shake the bottle and observe the changes that occur. Look, yellow and blue make green!

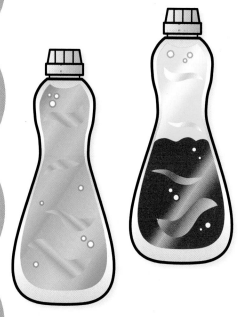

Patti Stuckemeyer
Effingham I Head Start
Effingham, IL

TEC61022

TEC61022

TEC61022

TEC61022

Lava Landscape

Your little ones will "lava" this land-scape that resembles the dinosaurs' land of long ago. To dye rice to fill your sand table, mix several drops of food coloring with enough rubbing alcohol to soak the amount of rice you would like to dye that color. Soak rice in each different color of alcohol you prepare. Drain the rice; then spread it out to dry. Add the colored rice to an empty sand table or tub along with toy dinosaurs. Watch out! This volcanic center could erupt with excitement.

Nancy Irgens
ICC Preschool
Violet Hill, AR

Sensory Pool

Entice students to experience the sense of touch in this unique center. Purchase a small inflatable pool that can be stored easily when not in use. Fill the pool with a variety of soft materials, such as cotton, foam packing peanuts, felt pieces, or stuffed animals. Have the children take off their shoes, jump in, and explore!

Kristen Sharpe
Kristen's Corner
Mansfield, MA

Dappling in Dentistry

Your little dentists will have fun drilling and filling at this sensory center. To prepare a cavity-filling mixture, add gray powdered-tempera paint to white glue until a thick paste is formed. Place a container of the glue mixture, craft sticks, and chunks of Styrofoam in your sensory table. Label your center with a sign if desired. Beforehand use a battery-powered screwdriver to have each child drill holes into the Styrofoam "teeth." Then have each child use a craft stick to fill the "cavities" with the glue mixture.

Susan Bowen
Community Christian Preschool
El Cajon, CA

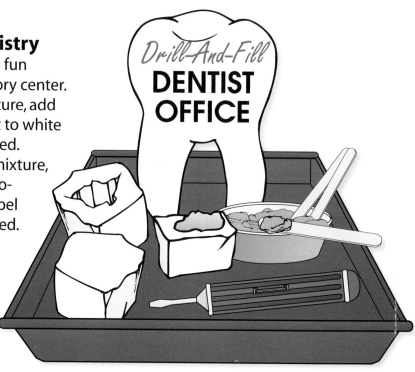

Seasonal Sensation

What's orange and black and creeping with spiders? The contents of your sensory table when you fill it with orange and black shredded paper (available at party-supply stores) and a quantity of plastic spiders. Encourage a child to find the spiders and then count them. Your little ones are sure to love this sensory-table surprise!

Susan Burbridge
Colonial Hills United Methodist School
San Antonio, TX

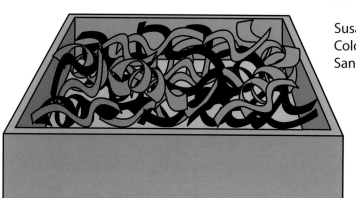

Hide-and-Seek

Your preschoolers will enthusiastically seek out this challenging fine-motor, matching, and counting center! Collect several different sets of ten objects, such as markers or crayons. (If desired, collect sets of seasonal items or items that relate to your current themes.) Label each of ten large index cards with a different numeral from 1 to 10 and a corresponding dot set. Hide the items in a sensory table filled with dry rice. Place the cards nearby.

To use this center, a child chooses a card, then searches for the corresponding number of one type of item in the rice. As he finds the items, he places them atop the dots on the card. When the card is full, he returns the items to the sensory table. He continues by choosing a new card. As a super sensory challenge, cover the rice container with a towel and then have the child search for objects using only his sense of touch.

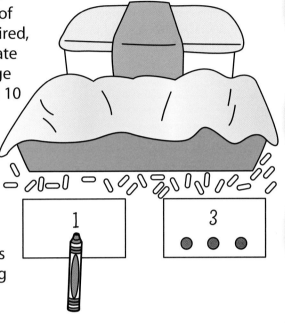

Egg Hunt

How can you provide an exciting egg hunt yet keep it manageable? Use your sensory table! Hide colorful pom-poms (for eggs) among lots of Easter grass. Have youngsters collect the little eggs in small baskets. If you have several different colors of baskets, hide pom-poms in the same colors. Then ask youngsters to sort the eggs by color, matching each one to the same color basket. When the hunt is over, invite the little egg hunters to hide the eggs for another group of friends to find!

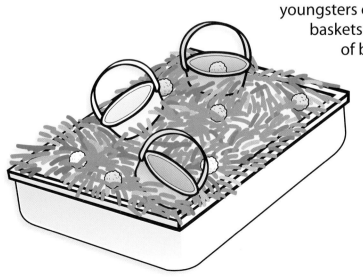

Amy Rain Monahan
Play Pals Program at Saint Anthony's
  Health Center
Alton, IL

Water & Sand

Road Construction

Your sensory area will be humming with the sounds of bulldozers and backhoes when you add some road-construction props. Fill your sensory table with soil. Add a supply of toy construction vehicles. Spray the soil with water to keep it moist and pliable; then watch your crew of workers dig in.

Claudia V. Tábora
Como Community Child Care,
Minneapolis, MN

Desert Dig

Sharpen your students' senses and skills by creating this simple, yet exciting, classroom desert. Hide an assortment of rocks, plastic lizards, and toy snakes in your sand table or in a large plastic tub filled with sand. If desired, add colored sand to the table or tub. Encourage your youngsters to research desert life by placing in the area several reference books about deserts, lizards, and snakes. Add magnifying glasses, small shovels, and sand sifters to help your little ones search the sand. Stock the area with crayons and paper so that students can draw pictures of their desert discoveries. After informing your little ones of the buried items, invite them to visit the area and use the provided materials.

Kathy Valeri
Spaulding Memorial, Townsend, MA

Octopus and Starfish Arms

Once they dive in, your students are sure to get stuck on this center! Obtain a rubber bath mat that has small suction cups on one side. Cut it into starfish shapes and strips (to resemble octopus arms). Add the shapes and strips to your water table. As students have fun experimenting with the suction cups, they'll learn how octopi and starfish move about and cling to objects. Don't be surprised if parents report that youngsters want to try this ocean critter with bath mats at home too!

Dina Fehler
Kirkland, WA

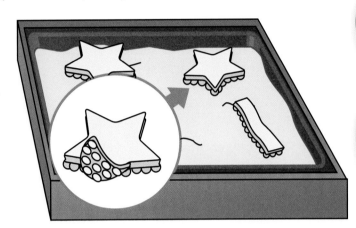

Blowin' in the Wind

Let wind blow sailboats across your water table. For each sailboat, staple one-half of a plastic straw to the inside of an empty margarine tub to create a boat and mast. Let children use crayons to decorate triangles of tagboard. Laminate these colorful sails; then staple each one to a straw mast. Place the sailboats in your water table and let your young sailors cast off!

Betty Silkunas
Lansdale, PA

Water & Sand

Spooky Water Shakers

Set these spooky shakers in your water table and it will be floating with fun. Remove the labels from several small, clear plastic water bottles with tops. Place some scary things—such as small rubber snakes, plastic bats, or plastic spiders—in the bottles. (You may want to invite your youngsters to assist you so that they will feel comfortable playing with the shakers.) Next add some green, purple, or black decorative grass and a little glitter to the bottles before filling them with water. Hot-glue the tops to the bottles. Finally, leave these spooky shakers bobbing in your water table for your youngsters to shake, spin, and swirl.

Dayle Timmons
Alimacani Elementary School
Jacksonville, FL

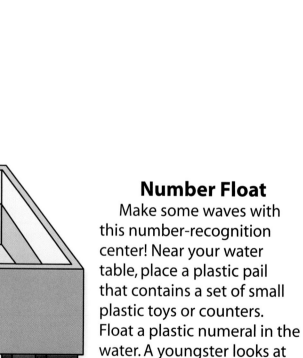

Number Float

Make some waves with this number-recognition center! Near your water table, place a plastic pail that contains a set of small plastic toys or counters. Float a plastic numeral in the water. A youngster looks at the numeral and then places a matching set of toys or counters in the water. It's a splash of counting fun!

Alphabet Quackers

Make a big splash with your little ones with this simple, yet fun, addition to your water table. Program the bottoms of a number of rubber-duck bath toys with numerals or letters. Float the ducks in your water table; then invite your little ones to take turns selecting a duck from the table and identifying the symbol written on it. As a challenge, have youngsters sequence the ducks by numeral or find ducks programmed with matching uppercase and lowercase letters. Be sure to invite the children to enjoy some free water play, too!

Lonnie Murphy
Sarasota, FL

Winter Water Wonders

Give your water table the deep freeze with these exciting winter additions. Fill miniature decorator cake pans with colored water and freeze them. Then add the frozen shapes to the water in the table. Add ice cubes and refreezable plastic ice cubes. If icicles are easily found in your area, add several of them as well. For added fun, place plastic Arctic-animal toys in the water. Brrr!

Water & Sand

Rainbow Ice

Is the ice melting outside? It'll be melting inside with this very colorful activity! To prepare, fill a bucket nearly full of water; then freeze it. Put the block of ice in your water table. Then prepare three containers of salted water: one red, one blue, and one yellow. Have your students use eyedroppers to drop the colored water onto the ice block. Have them observe how the salt water melts the ice, creating craters in the ice block. They'll also see how the colors of water blend to create new shades. Cool!

JoAnn Brukiewa
St. Clare School
Baltimore, MD

Water-Table Fun

Enrich your water table with this cool idea. Halfway fill your empty water table with ice cubes. Place several pairs of rubber gloves near the table. To use this center, a child puts on the rubber gloves and creates the design of his choice with the ice cubes. For example, he may make an ice castle or an ice house—or he may simply wish to slide the cubes on the table.

Betty Silkunas, Lansdale, PA

Laundry Table

Set your water table outside and convert it into a laundry table. Half-fill the table with warm water; then add a scoop of mild laundry soap. In a laundry basket near the table, provide clothespins and small cloth items such as old handkerchiefs, doll clothing, and socks. Mount a clothesline between two chairs near the table, or set up a clothes-drying rack. To use this center, a child takes a piece of clothing from the laundry basket and washes it in the laundry table. (If desired, add an additional tub of water for rinsing.) He then wrings the excess water from the piece of clothing and uses a clothespin to clip it to the clothesline. Rub-a-dub-dub!

Color Dig

Practice color-matching skills with this sand-table activity. Collect two empty sanitized egg cartons and 24 rocks that fit in the eggcups. Choose 12 colors you'd like students to learn. Paint two rocks and two sections of the egg cartons with each of the colors. When the rocks have dried, hide them in your sand table. Have students go on a color dig to hunt for the rocks and match them to the correct sections of the egg cartons.

Carolyn M. Patterson
Grove City Head Start
Grove City, PA

Water & Sand

Digging Up Bones

Youngsters will uncover their archeological skills when digging up these bones. During a study of dinosaurs, hide bone-shaped dog treats in your indoor and outdoor sand centers. Provide youngsters with buckets, shovels, and even paintbrushes to aid them in their digging.

Antares Narizzano
Rainbow Station Child
    Development Center
Richmond, VA

Like Sand in an Hourglass...

Reuse an empty two-liter plastic soda bottle by turning it into a discovery toy for your sand or rice center. To make one, cut off the top third of a bottle. Invert the top portion of the bottle; then insert it into the bottom portion as shown. Tape the portions together, being sure to cover any rough edges. Encourage students to pour sand or rice into the funnel and watch as it fills the container. If desired cut a window on the side of the bottle for better peeking and faster emptying.

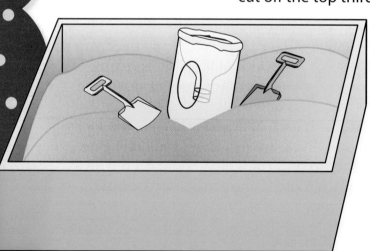

Heather Snider
Oklahoma City, OK

Down and Dirty

Get the dirt on a unique sensory experience for the sand table—plastic creepy crawlers buried in soil! Partially fill your sand table with loose soil. Collect a supply of plastic critters—such as spiders and insects—and add them to the dirt. Add shovels and suggest that little ones get down and dirty! Be sure to have some disposable wipes available for temporary cleanup until students can get to the sink for a thorough handwashing.

Jane Brom-Pierzina, KinderCare District 1 and 2
Minnetonka, MN

Frosty the Sandman

Try this idea for sandy "snow" in your sensory table! Add enough water to the sand to make it stick together like snow. Complete the center with ice-cream scoops, melon ballers, bowls, and other nifty circular objects. Students will develop their fine-motor skills as they make snowballs, mold snowpeople, and create snow sculptures in the sand. The best part about this tactile experience is that nothing melts!

Betty Silkunas
Lansdale, PA

Water & Sand

Baskets Full of Fun!

Enrich your sand table with this hands-on idea. Half-fill your table with colored plastic grass. Place several baskets, small plastic chicks and bunnies, and plastic eggs in the grass. To use this center, have little ones use the materials provided to create nifty spring baskets!

Mary Borreca
Martinsville, TX

An Archeological Dig

Exciting exploration and discoveries await your youngsters when you transform your sand table into the site of an archeological dig. To prepare for the dig, collect pictures from magazines (such as *National Geographic*) of actual archeological digs. Also cut out the pictures of jewels and coins on page 67. Laminate and cut out the pictures; then hide them in the sand. Also supply digging tools, plastic baskets for sifting the sand, and brushes for carefully dusting sand from the treasures. Share and discuss with the class the pictures of the actual digs. Then encourage children to visit their archeological site.

Susan Ahlhorn, Wee Wuns Preschool
Cypress, TX

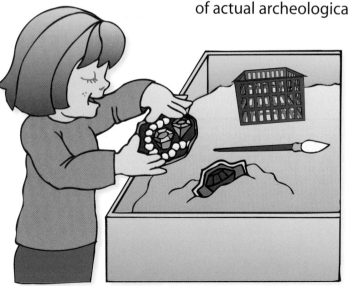

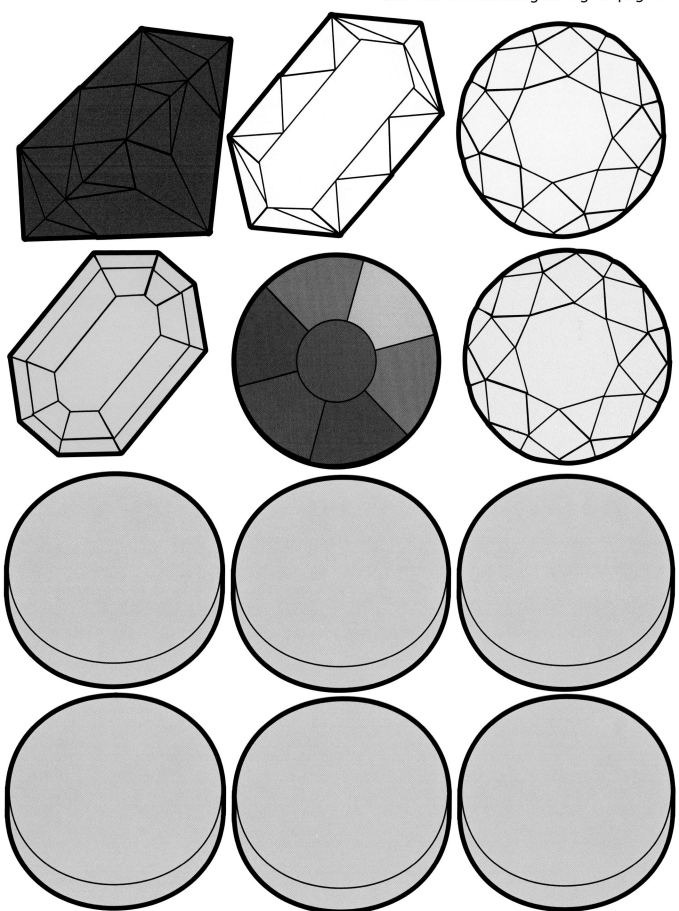

TEC61022

TEC61022

TEC61022

TEC61022

TEC61022

TEC61022

TEC61022

TEC61022

TEC61022

TEC61022

TEC61022

TEC61022

Preschoolers in the Pool

Preschoolers will love the water in this pool! To set up this **cutting** activity, toss some blue and green crepe paper streamers and scraps of blue and green construction paper in a child's plastic swimming pool. Add some plastic or vinyl fish that can "swim" in the water. Then put two pairs of scissors in a beach bucket nearby. Encourage pairs of youngsters to sit in the pool and snip away. Remind them not to "splash" the scraps while they practice cutting!

Stephanie Jagoda, Rountree Elementary, Allen, TX
Jill Simon, Poland Boardman Childcare Center, Poland, OH

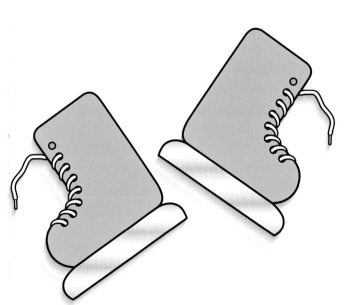

Lacing Up Skates

Here's the perfect place for little ones to warm up their **lacing skills!** Trace an ice skate template (pattern on page 76) on poster board two times. Cut out the shapes and glue foil atop each blade. If desired, laminate the shapes for durability. Then punch out the holes along the front edge of each skate cutout. On the back of each skate, near the toe, securely tape one end of a shoelace. Youngsters can glide over for lacing practice time after time!

Lizanne Mullins
The Harmony School
Basking Ridge, NJ

Fine Motor & Gross Motor

Wild Card

This animal **lacing** card is "sew" wild! To make one, use the pattern on page 77 to cut a zebra shape from white poster board. After adding facial details, use a hole puncher to punch holes as shown. Dip the ends of a long length of black yarn into school glue; then let the glue harden overnight. Thread the yarn through one hole and tie the end of the yarn to the sewing card. Then invite a child to lace the yarn through the holes to create stripes for the zebra.

Diana Kraft
Growing Vines Playschool
Arusha, Tanzania

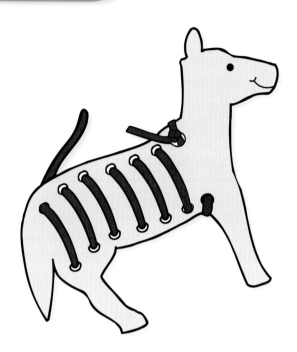

Salad Time

Give youngsters an opportunity to create an enticing salad while developing **fine-motor skills.** Stock the center with scalloped sheets of green paper in various shades to represent lettuce. Add an assortment of construction paper vegetable-shaped cutouts, play dough, scissors, and plastic bowls.

To make a salad, a student tears the green paper into "bite-size" pieces and puts them in a bowl. She then uses scissors to cut up her choice of vegetable cutouts to add to her salad. If any other vegetables or toppings are desired, encourage her to mold these from play dough, then use them to garnish her salad.

If desired, invite the child to carry her salad over to the housekeeping center. Provide empty salad-dressing bottles, tongs, and plastic forks for a pretend feast. These salads are scrumptious skill builders, any way you toss them!

Linda Blassingame
JUST 4&5 Developmental Laboratory
Mobile, AL

Rocket Bowling

Youngsters will have fun to spare when they participate in this space-themed bowling game that exercises **motor skills and counting skills!** Begin by making ten rocket-shaped bowling pins. To make one, cut a 3"x 3"x 3½" triangle from tagboard or lightweight cardboard. Then cut two opposing slits in one end of a cardboard tube. Slip the triangle cutout into the slits until the 3½" edge is even with the bottom of the tube. Then use a marker to decorate the tube to resemble a rocket. Next, make an asteroid bowling ball by wrapping duct tape around a three-inch Styrofoam ball. Set up the ten rocket pins and bowling ball in your gross-motor area. Invite each child to go rocket bowling and then have him count the number of rockets he knocks down. Strike!

Terri Maass
Lynchburg, VA

Flower Toss

This beanbag **tossing** game reinforces colors just in time for spring! Collect a number of colorful round plastic baskets. Secure the bottom of each basket to the center of a matching paper flower shape. Add paper stems and leaves if desired. Arrange the flower baskets on the floor of an open area. Then give a child several beanbags and encourage him to pick the flowers in which he would like to toss the bags. It's a gross-motor garden!

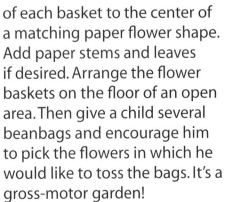

Audrey Englehardt
Meadowbrook Elementary School
Moro, IL

Fine Motor & Gross Motor

Play-Dough Placemats

Use these placemats to protect tabletops and to identify personal space when using **play dough.** To make a set of play-dough placemats, copy the placemats on pages 78 and 79 onto tagboard. Then laminate the mats. When a child visits the center, encourage him to form play dough into the shapes on each mat.

Susan Burbridge
Colonial Hills United Methodist
   School
San Antonio, TX

Counting Candles

Everyone loves birthdays! Invite youngsters at your **play dough** center to create birthday cakes. Cut out the number cards on page 41 and place them at the center. Have each child take a card and add the corresponding number of birthday candles to her cake. For even more fun, use real birthday cards instead of number cards.

Destiny Simms
Kiddie Academy Learning Centers
Laurel, MD

72

Fine Motor & Gross Motor

Many-Eyed Monsters

There's something monstrously fun afoot at this **play dough** center! Invite little ones to shape play dough into monsters— any shapes will do! Also encourage them to shape varying colors of play dough into eyeballs of assorted sizes for their monsters. Then ask each child to count the number of eyes his monster has. Have him compare his monster's eyes to the eyes of a friend's monster. Which monster has more? Are the eyes the same colors? The same sizes? It's a marvelous mixture of monsters and math!

Kristen Shoemake
Clairbourn School
San Gabriel, CA

Flower Garden

Fine-motor skills will be in bloom when you set up this flowery **play dough** center. To prepare, stock the center with small clear plastic cups, green craft sticks, and a supply of pipe cleaners cut in half. To use the center, a child places some play dough in a cup, places a small ball of dough on one end of a craft stick, and then inserts the other end into the cup. Next, she uses the pipe cleaners to create flower petals and inserts them into the ball of dough. Encourage the child to use the materials to create a variety of flowers.

adapted from an idea by Betsy Gaynor
Creative Nursery School
Naperville, IL

Pumpkin Pie Play Dough

This yummy-smelling dough is sure to add spice to your **play dough** area! Place a batch of this scented dough and some white play dough in your center. Add some fall cookie cutters, small pie tins, and rolling pins to the area. Invite your little ones to make fall cookies. Or encourage them to make play-dough pumpkin pies, using the white dough for crust and the scented dough for filling. Encourage your little bakers to make as many pastries as they want, but remind them that these goodies only smell good. No tasting please!

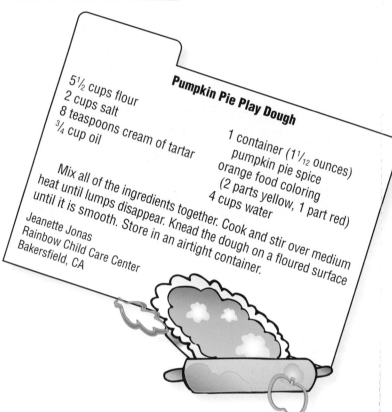

Pumpkin Pie Play Dough

5½ cups flour
2 cups salt
8 teaspoons cream of tartar
¾ cup oil

1 container (1½₁₂ ounces) pumpkin pie spice
orange food coloring (2 parts yellow, 1 part red)
4 cups water

Mix all of the ingredients together. Cook and stir over medium heat until lumps disappear. Knead the dough on a floured surface until it is smooth. Store in an airtight container.

Jeanette Jonas
Rainbow Child Care Center
Bakersfield, CA

Peppy Play Dough

Add an exciting aroma to your **play dough** too? Just add a few drops of peppermint oil or extract (and red food coloring, if desired) to your favorite play-dough recipe. When children go to this center, encourage them to identify the new smell. Provide rolling pins and candy cane–shaped cookie cutters to cut out the peppermint dough. Mmmm—smells sweet!

Fine Motor & Gross Motor

A Box of Chocolates

Treat yourself (or your coworkers) to candies in a heart-shaped box; then place the empty box and candy wrappers at your **play dough** center. Add a batch of this luscious-looking play dough and watch your little ones use their fine-motor skills to roll out some confections! Encourage children to count aloud as they put one play-dough chocolate in each wrapper. (Make sure youngsters know that this dough is not edible!)

Rosalie Sumsion
Monument Valley, UT

Chocolate-Scented Play Dough

1¼ cups flour
½ cup cocoa powder
½ cup salt
½ tablespoon cream of tartar
1½ tablespoons cooking oil
1 cup boiling water

Mix the dry ingredients. Add the oil and boiling water. Stir quickly, mixing well. When cool, mix with your hands. Store in an airtight container.

Hamburger Helpers

Celebrate summer with this sizzlin' **play dough** center. Provide a wire baking rack to represent a grill. Then add other props—such as an apron, a checkered tablecloth, paper plates, waxed paper, a hamburger press, a spatula, and empty condiment squeeze bottles—to create an atmosphere of short-order fun. Be sure to include several colors of play dough for children to use when making char-broiled burgers with all the toppings, such as green lettuce, red tomatoes, and yellow cheese.

Skate Pattern

Use with "Lacing Up Skates" on page 69.

TEC61022

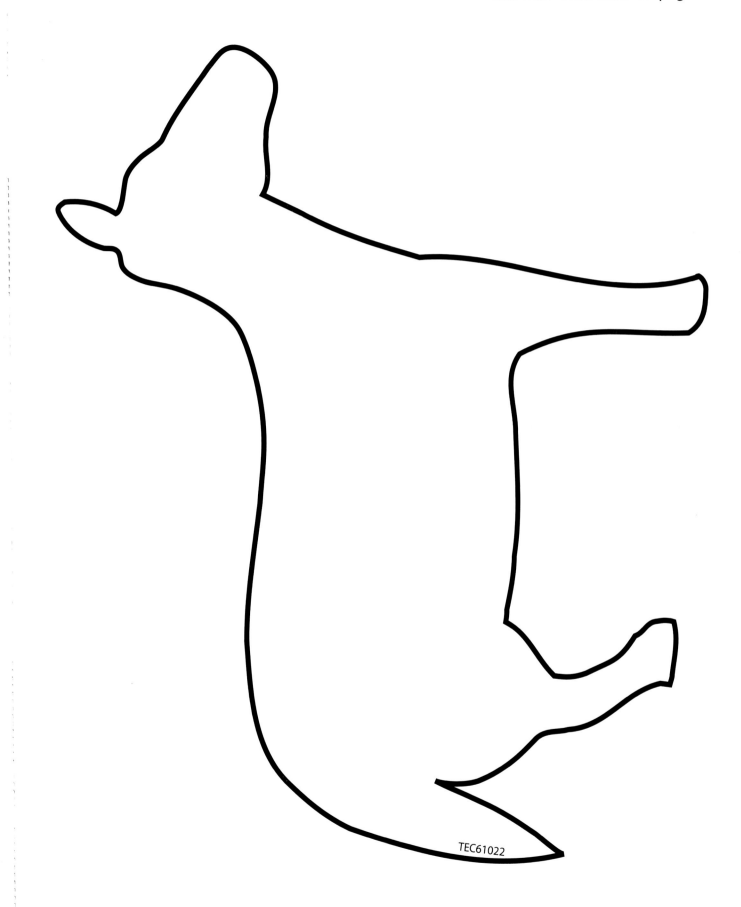

TEC61022

Play-Dough Placemat

Use with "Play-Dough Placemats" on page 72.

©The Mailbox® • *Learning Centers* • TEC61022

Fall Leaf Paintings

Use those beautiful leaves your preschoolers pick up on nature walks for this painting activity. Have each child tape a few leaves onto a sheet of paper. Attach the paper to your easel; then invite the child to paint the entire paper with orange and yellow paint. When the paint dries, remove the leaves and look at the design that's left behind!

Angie Jenkins
Love to Learn
Knoxville, TN

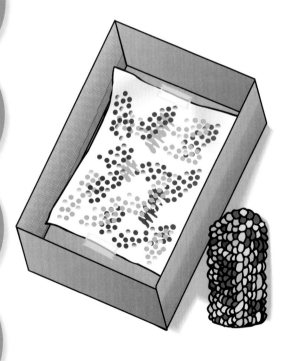

Corn on a Roll

Preschoolers will fall for this seasonal painting technique! To prepare, purchase some ornamental corn and break the cobs in half. Then tape a sheet of paper into the bottom of a shallow box. Dip a cob half into fall-colored tempera paint; then place it in the box. Have a child tilt the box to make the corn roll around, creating an interesting design. Repeat the painting with more fall colors for some striking seasonal artwork!

Nola Surmanek
First United Methodist Child Enrichment Center
Hyattsville, MD

Snowflake Flurry

These wintry snowflakes are sure to get flurries of attention. To prepare, mix a small amount of liquid dish detergent in the paint at your art center. Next, place a supply of aluminum foil sheets near the area. Help each child clip a sheet of foil to an easel; then invite her to paint snow-flakes on the foil. When the paint is dry, mount the foil on a sheet of construction paper. Hang these painted wonders near windows to create an awesome flurry of flakes. If desired, invite little ones to use hand mirrors to explore the light and color reflected from the foil.

Dawn Hurley
CUMC Child Care Center
Bethel Park, PA

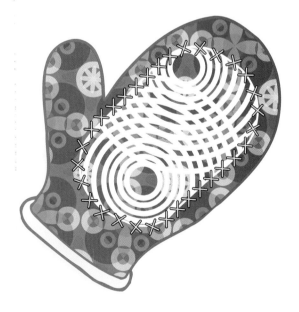

Textured Mittens

If you have some mittens that have lost their mates, don't throw them out! Recycle them for your painting center. Sew a patch of lace, dust mop, sponge, or another interest-ing textured material to the palm of a mitten. Invite youngsters to slip on a mitten, dip it into paint, and make prints on paper. When the painting is through, wash the mittens and hang them up to dry for more painting fun later!

Nancy Kaczvowski
ECFE/SR
Luverne, MN

Cool Collages

Promote your students' free expression in their artwork by adding tactile materials to your paint center. For example, during February, hang on an easel a bag containing pieces of red, white, and pink tissue paper; cellophane wrap; yarn; and doilies. Have each of your little ones paint a picture, then press her choice of objects in the wet paint to create a collage. The creative process gets a workout here!

Bernadette Hoyer
McGinn and Coles Schools
Scotch Plains, NJ

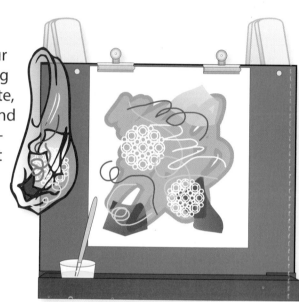

Carrot Painting

This spring, break away from brushes and try painting with produce! Set out your painting cups with a raw carrot tucked into each one. Encourage youngsters to paint and draw with the pointed ends of the carrots instead of fingers or brushes. Then display their "24-carrot" creations for everyone to admire!

Shelley Hoster
Jack and Jill Early Learning Center
Norcross, GA

Rose Print Bouquets

This center idea is so simple, yet it provides bouquets of painting fun! Simply stock your art area with silk roses and shallow pans of tempera paint. If desired, add a few drops of rose potpourri oil or perfume to the paint. Invite children who visit the center to dip the roses into the paint and then press them onto large sheets of paper to create rose prints. Everything is coming up roses!

Jenny Anderson
Algonquin, IL

Sarah's Bug

Designer Bugs

Creepy, crawly critters are everywhere in springtime, but most likely you've never seen bugs like these! Cut various head, thorax, and abdomen shapes from sponges and prepare each one for stamping. Place the stampers, shallow containers of tempera paint, and white construction paper at the center. Next, help each child mix and match the body parts to sponge-paint a bug of her own design. When the paint is dry, have her use a marker to add legs, antennae, and wings as desired. Then invite her to show her critter to the class and tell a story about it!

Sue Fleischmann
Waukesha County Project Head Start
Waukesha, WI

Picnic Art

Make painting a real picnic with this idea! Cover a table with a vinyl red-and-white-checkered tablecloth. Set out plastic ketchup and mustard bottles filled with red and yellow tempera paint. Then fill an old set of salt and pepper shakers with white and black sand. (Make your own colored sand by mixing powdered tempera paint with clean play sand.) Then set a white paper plate at each place, and watch the squirting and shaking begin as your youngsters create picnic art!

Cathy Consford
Buda Primary Early Learning Center
Buda, TX

Seashell Sensation

Bring the seashore to the art center by making each of your youngsters a shell to paint. Obtain a collection of clamshells and a package of modeling compound. (Or mix a batch of your favorite clay.) To make a shell for each child, press the clay onto the outside of a shell. Peel it off, reshape it, and then trim around the edges of the resulting shape. Once the shell replicas have hardened, hide them in a tub of sand located near the art center. Invite each student to use a shovel and a paintbrush to find and clean one shell. Encourage him to paint his shell and then set it aside to dry. Display this one-of-a-kind seashell collection on a sandy tabletop for all to admire!

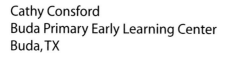

Bonnie McKenzie
Cheshire Country Day School
Cheshire, CT

Festive Flags

Celebrate Flag Day at your art center with some creative red, white, and blue designs. Place large sheets of white paper at your easel, along with large brushes and red, white, and blue tempera paint. Encourage youngsters to paint their own flag designs for a patriotic display in the classroom.

Bernadette Hoyer
McGinn and Coles Schools
Scotch Plains, NJ

The Great Paint Scrape

Your preschoolers are destined to make unique designs when you place these scrapers at your painting center. To make the scrapers, use pinking shears or scallop-edged scissors to cut a supply of plastic lids in half. Drop a spoonful of paint on a sheet of paper and have a child use a scraper to swirl, smear, and spread the paint. For more interesting designs, squirt different colors of paint on the paper and have the child use the scraper to blend the colors. Your little ones will love exploring the different lines and patterns of these colorful designs!

Jill Beattie
Apple Place Nursery School, Chambersburg, PA

Carolyn Kramer
Vienna Baptist Children's Center, Vienna, VA

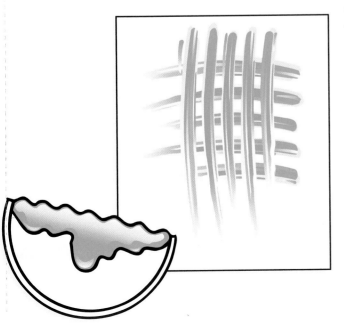

Art

Cool Paint Trays

Help little ones explore color mixing with the help of some ice cube trays. Give each child an ice cube tray. Squirt two colors of tempera paint into a compartment of the tray; then invite the child to mix the paints with her brush and paint with the newfound color. Continue with other color combinations in other compartments of the tray.

Deborah Oesterling
Sterling Academy, Cary, NC

A Cookie Sheet Palette

Looking for easy-to-use painting materials? Look in the kitchen! First, fold a few paper towels so that they fit on the bottom of a cookie sheet. Squirt liquid tempera paint in two different colors onto the paper towels. Place a sheet of art paper on another cookie sheet. Invite a child at this center to press cookie cutters onto the paint-soaked paper towels and then press them onto the paper to make prints. Encourage her to keep going until she has a whole tray of yummy-looking cookies!

Cynthia Sayman
All My Children Daycare Center
Binghamton, NY

Salad-Spinner Art

Take an old salad spinner out of the kitchen and into the classroom for some painting fun! Place paper in the bottom of a salad spinner. (Use one without drainage holes in the outer tub, to avoid any mess.) Then put in the colander insert. Drop in a bit of paint and add a touch of glitter, if you like. Then put the top in place and invite a child to make the paint spin! The mess will stay inside the tub, and the painting will be "spin-tacular"!

Nancy Morgan
Bremerton, WA

Puppy Stamp

Youngsters can stamp to their hearts' content with this adaptable activity. To prepare, make a supply of the puppy pattern on page 88. Then place them at a center along with several related rubber stamps, an inkpad, and crayons. To use this center, a child chooses a puppy to color and stamp as desired.

Samita Arora
Rainbows United, Inc.
Wichita, KS

Puppy Pattern
Use with "Puppy Stamp" on page 87.

TEC61022

That's Me!

Bring some friendly faces to your blocks center when you make these fun photo cylinders! To make one, take a full-body photograph of a child; then cut out the child's body from the developed photo. Next, cover a cardboard tube with construction paper or colored Con-Tact paper. Glue the cutout photo to the toilet paper tube; then cover the tube with a strip of clear Con-Tact paper for durability. Place each child's cylinder in the blocks area and invite your preschoolers to build structures for these familiar faces.

Dayle Timmons
Jacksonville Beach, FL

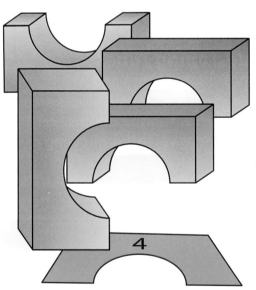

Block Buildup

Math skills will really stack up with this constructive idea. Trace blocks of a variety of shapes and sizes onto pieces of construction paper; then program each shape with a different numeral. Cut out the shapes; then laminate them for durability. Tape the cutouts to the floor of your block area. Challenge youngsters to build block towers that correspond to each cutout's shape and numeral. This center is a blockbuster!

Maggie Woldum
Head Start Preschool
Bozeman, MT

Blocks

Maze Table

Add a table to your block area for this "a-maze-ing" activity! Use wooden blocks to create a twisting pathway along the table, wide enough for a Ping-Pong ball to pass through. Then set a Ping-Pong ball at one end. A child at this center blows through his own individual drinking straw to propel the ball along the path and through the maze. What fun!

Betsy Fuhrmann
Dodds School
Springfield, IL

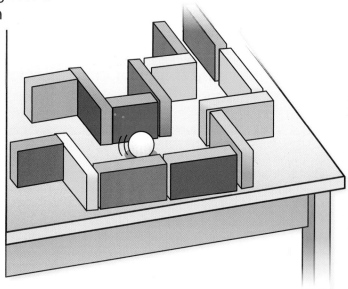

Telescoping Tubes

A collection of cardboard tubes and small balls will add fun and science to your blocks area! Gather cardboard tubes in various lengths and widths, including paper towel tubes, gift wrap tubes, mailing tubes—even carpet tubes! Add bouncing balls, golf balls, and Ping-Pong balls. Then encourage youngsters to place blocks under the tubes and experiment with varying angles as they send balls through them. It's full-tilt fun!

Linda Bille—Riviera United Methodist Preschool
Redondo Beach, CA

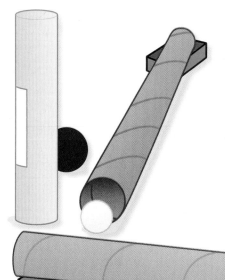

A House for Me

These charming additions to your block area will help youngsters learn their addresses as well as develop the concept of community. Purchase a class supply plus some extra of freestanding wooden house shapes (available at craft stores). Invite each child to paint a house; then allow the paint to dry. Use a permanent marker to write each child's name and address on her house. Then add the houses and a supply of toy vehicles to your block area. Encourage youngsters to build neighborhoods; then, as the children play, point out the names and addresses on the houses. Later add additional houses painted to resemble other familiar places, such as your preschool, stores, and fast-food restaurants. What a busy neighborhood!

Liz Novak, Pumpkin Patch Preschool And Playcare, Davenport, IA

"Dino-mite" Building

The fun won't become extinct at your block area when you add these prehistoric props. Collect a supply of sterilized egg cartons; then cut the top off each one. Encourage youngsters who visit the block area to arrange the egg cartons atop block caves to resemble stalactites. Prepare foliage for the environment by attaching paper palm fronds to one end of each of several cardboard tubes. Little ones' imaginations are sure to take them back in time when they're playing at this fun center.

Charlet Keller
ICC Preschool
Violet Hill, AR

Blocks

Homemade Blocks

Detergent boxes of all sizes make lightweight but sturdy blocks for your little ones. Simply gather the empty boxes, tape them closed, and wrap them with colorful Con-Tact covering. Let the building begin!

Sue Brewer
First Stages Daycare
Sharon, TN

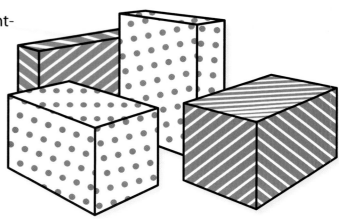

Prop Building

Flannelboard characters in the block area? Sure! Cut out the storybook characters on pages 97 and 99. Tape the character cutouts to rectangular blocks and add them to the block area. These freestanding block characters will encourage your little stagehands to build scenery—such as a house, bridge, or castle—and retell favorite stories their own special way!

Terri Wimpee
Dobbs Elementary
Rockwall, TX

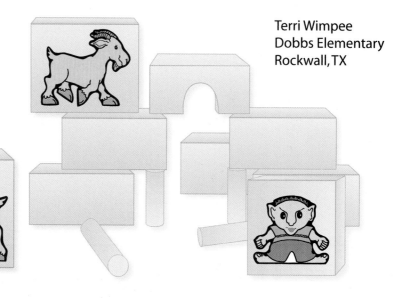

Creative Block Fun

Give your block center a new twist with this fun idea. Purchase several yards of different-colored, sheer gauzy fabric. Cut the fabric into a variety of sizes. Encourage youngsters who build houses in the center to drape the fabric pieces over the blocks to make doors or windows. Let their imaginations be their guide!

Amy Laubis
Children's Garden Preschool
Kenton, OH

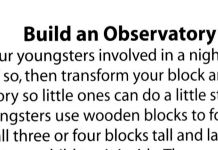

Build an Observatory

Are your youngsters involved in a nighttime theme? If so, then transform your block area into an observatory so little ones can do a little stargazing. Have youngsters use wooden blocks to form a circle with a wall three or four blocks tall and large enough for at least one child to sit inside. Then create a telescope by covering a paper-towel tube with yellow construction paper. Decorate it with star and moon stickers. Place the imaginary telescope inside your observatory. To provide students with some stars to gaze at, cut star shapes from sheets of foil wrapping paper glued to sheets of tagboard. Suspend the stars from your classroom ceiling using yarn or fishing line. Invite students to visit the center and take turns with the telescope. Twinkle, twinkle!

Charlet Keller
ICC Preschool
Violet Hill, AR

Blocks

Neighborhood Boxes

What's new around the neighborhood? Buildings for your block area! Collect boxes in a variety of sizes and shapes such as jewelry boxes, shoeboxes, and milk cartons. Have youngsters paint the boxes with tempera paints. Then have them use markers and construction paper to add features such as windows and doors. Help the children label the buildings to denote a purpose for each one—gas station, hospital, post office, school, police station, etc. Then invite your young community planners to go to town in the block center!

Nancy Slotnick
The Kids' Space
Braintree, MA

Floor "Mat-tropolis"

Keep things moving at your blocks center by adding this easy-to-make floor mat that represents Your Town, USA! Using permanent markers, draw roads, buildings, and natural landmarks on a vinyl, felt-backed tablecloth (available at discount stores). Put the mat on the floor of your blocks center. Then encourage children visiting the center to use toy vehicles and blocks to get the city bustling with activity.

Maureen F. Guerin
Hilltop Learning Center
Tewksbury, MA

Tabletop Town

Enhance your block area with a tabletop town cut from felt. Begin by cutting a large piece of felt to fit on a tabletop. Cut additional colors of felt into strips to create a maze of roads that can be placed on the larger piece of felt. Also cut out felt trees, houses, and other buildings if desired. Decorate the felt pieces with slick or puffy fabric paint. Little ones will love setting up the town and driving toy cars and trucks along its roadways.

Sharon Otto
SRI/St. Elizabeth Child Development Center
Lincoln, NE

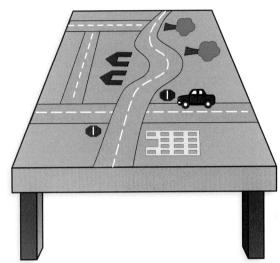

Road Map

Your students will be on the road to lots of fun when you create streets in your block area. Use wide masking tape to lay out a series of roads on the floor or carpet. Leave room between roads for students to build block houses and buildings. Add to the fun by laminating paper cutouts of road signs. Tape each sign to a toothpick and insert the pick into an inverted section cut from an egg carton. Place the signs along the roadsides and let little ones "drive" their toy cars and trucks on the masking-tape roadways.

Donna Leonard
Head Start
Dyersville, IA

Blocks

Tending the Garden

Cultivate the roots of your little ones' imaginations with this fun garden idea. Encourage students to make garden rows with blocks. Provide an assortment of plastic vegetables for the children to "plant" around, on top of, and under the blocks. Have children's garden tools and baskets nearby for the harvest. There is sure to be lots of class-grown fun in this bountiful block garden. Don't be surprised if a produce stand is the next thing in demand!

Linda Blassingame
JUST 4 & 5 Developmental Laboratory
Mobile, AL

Box Snowpal

Building an indoor snowpal is so cool! Use white paper to cover three boxes— one small, one medium, and one large. Poke two holes in opposite sides of the medium- size box and slide a wooden dowel through the holes for arms. Then attach the hook side of small pieces of self-adhesive Velcro fastening tape to the boxes so that pom- pom eyes and felt cutouts (a nose, a mouth, and several buttons) can be attached. Also provide scarves, hats, and pairs of mittens or gloves. Little ones will have a grand time stacking the boxes from largest to smallest and adding snowpal particulars. "Brrr-illiant"!

Jean Young
Lake Orion Community Schools
Lake Orion, MI

96

TEC61022

TEC61022

TEC61022

TEC61022

TEC61022

TEC61022

TEC61022

100

Farmer's Market

Enhance a harvest theme by inviting your young farmers to pretend they are running a farmer's market in your dramatic-play area. Provide bushel baskets of plastic fruits and vegetables, a balance scale, a toy cash register, shopping baskets, and a supply of paper bags. Add some plaid shirts and bandanas for dress-up, along with empty purses and wallets. Model how to play the parts of the farmer selling her produce and the customer choosing and buying. Then have youngsters start harvesting the fun!

Rhonda Yates
Paso Robles, CA

Clip Those Coupons!

If your preschoolers enjoy having a grocery store in your dramatic-play area, add this twist to develop math and motor skills! Ask parents to donate the coupon sections from your local paper. Put the coupon sections in a shallow box, with several pairs of safety scissors nearby. Invite youngsters to clip coupons before they begin their shopping trips at your imaginary store! Try to stock up on empty containers for items shown on the coupons so your young shoppers can put their matching skills to the test too!

Andrea Henderson
Jefferson Brethren Preschool
Goshen, IN

Dramatic Play

Hamburgers, Anyone?

Use this idea to transform your dramatic-play area into a fast-food restaurant. In advance, visit a local fast-food restaurant and request donations of paper bags and unused burger boxes or paper wrappers. Next, cut out bun shapes from sponges, and hamburger patty shapes and toppings from craft foam. Place all of the supplies in the center. Then invite youngsters to take turns making burgers. If desired, use your puppet theater to create a drive-through window for your restaurant. Add a few tricycles and you're ready for business!

Lisa Dukes
Wee Ones Preschool
Pflugerville, TX

Nancy M. Lotzer
Farmer's Branch, TX

Grocery Shopping Lists

Sooner or later you'll want to set up a grocery store in your dramatic-play area. When you do, be sure to provide these rebus-style shopping lists. They'll extend the dramatic play in your center while promoting language and literacy skills at the same time. To prepare each list, cut out the grocery cards on page 113. Glue the pictures onto construction paper, label the list, and then laminate it. What's on your list? I'm looking for bananas, cereal, and milk!

Karen Still
Chevy Chase United Methodist Church Preschool
Chevy Chase, MD

Preschool Posy Shop

Your children's color-recognition, sorting, and counting skills are sure to bloom when you transform your dramatic-play area into a posy shop! Ask parents to donate old artificial flowers, vases, and flowerpots; then place the items in your center along with seed packets, paper, markers, and play money. Encourage children playing in the center to count the flowers and sort them by color. Also encourage literacy by having workers make price tags and signs for the store. Now that's some bloomin' good fun!

Colleen Keller
Clarion-Goldfield Elementary
Clarion, IA

Flower Arranging

Creativity will be in bloom at your dramatic-play center when you add some oatmeal-canister vases! To make one, cover an oatmeal canister with Con-Tact covering. Snap the plastic lid on; then use a pencil to poke holes in the lid. Provide an assortment of artificial flowers and invite youngsters to insert the stems into the holes in the canister lid. Ta da—instant flower arrangements that are easy enough for little hands!

Mary Kay Vidmar
St. Rose Catholic School
Wilmington, IL

Dramatic Play

Medical Center

If you're doing a unit on body awareness, why not transform your dramatic play area into a medical center for a few weeks? Decorate the walls with posters donated by a local doctor's office. Provide a white, button-up shirt to serve as a doctor's coat. Then add props such as a toy doctor's kit (with a stethoscope, a thermometer, a reflex hammer, and other tools), wrap-style bandages, and cotton balls. Include a clipboard, pencils, and pads of paper for filling out forms and writing prescriptions. Your young physicians and their patients will love it!

Jennifer Barton
Elizabeth Green School
Newington, CT

SHOE SHOP

If the Shoe Fits...

Little ones won't recognize your housekeeping area when you convert it into a shoe store. Stock your center with a supply of shoeboxes—each box filled with a different pair of shoes. Also provide the center with low floor mirrors, a foot-measuring tool, paper bags, and a toy cash register. To the front of the center, tape a sign that reads "The Shoe Shop." To use the center, have little ones take turns being salespeople and customers.

Cathie Pesa
Youngstown City Schools
Boardman, OH

Visiting the Vet

Celebrate National Pet Week (typically at the beginning of May) by converting your dramatic play area into a veterinarian clinic. Bring in pet carriers or cut boxes to resemble animal cages. Put a toy doctor's kit in the area as well as other props—such as masks, rubber gloves, paper, pencils, and a clipboard. Also include a roll of gauze and an elastic bandage wrap for treating the "injured." Invite youngsters to bring stuffed animals from home to fill the clinic with patients. (Be sure to tag each toy pet with its owner's name.) Is there a doctor in the house?

Colleen Keller
Clarion-Goldfield Elementary, Clarion, IA

What Should I Pack?

Help your little ones pack for imaginary excursions with this handy luggage. To make suitcases, cover handled detergent boxes with colorful Con-Tact covering. Place the boxes in your housekeeping area along with small clothing articles and various travel items—such as sunglasses, empty film canisters, and empty trial-size containers. For added fun, include items for cold-weather lovers, too, so that youngsters will get some critical-thinking practice while packing for their getaways. Bon voyage!

Crystal Sirmans
Child Care Contacts R & R
Milledgeville, GA

Dramatic Play

Preschool Haircutters

Your students won't recognize the dramatic play area when you convert it into a hair salon. Glue photos of children (preferably your students) with different hair styles to sheets of construction paper. Also mount pictures of blow-dryers, scissors, and hair supplies on separate sheets of construction paper; then laminate the pages. Place the pages between two tagboard covers and bind the pages to make a book. Write the name of the hair salon on the cover of the book. Place the book, chairs, mirrors, empty shampoo bottles, towels, rollers, barrettes, ribbons, combs or brushes, and empty hairspray bottles in the center. Also stock the center with Styrofoam heads (used by beauticians) and several wigs. To the front of the center, tape a sign that reads "The Preschool Haircutters." To use the center, have little ones pretend to be barbers or beauticians. Wash and set?

Karen Eiben
The Kid's Place
La Salle, IL

An Office Visit

Keep children interested in your dramatic play area by transforming a traditional housekeeping center into an office setting. Add props such as an old computer keyboard or typewriter, a telephone, a phone book, a clipboard, a stapler, a hole puncher, rubber stamps, a stamp pad, notepads, pens, and pencils. Introduce students to the new equipment and discuss how the various items could be used. Your professional pretenders will love this center!

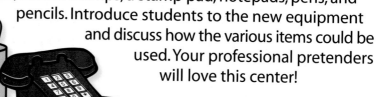

Jennifer Barton
Elizabeth Green School
Newington, CT

Happy Trails to You!

Saddle up and head for the Wild West—it's just across the room in your dramatic-play center! Cover the furniture in your housekeeping area with green fabric to resemble bushes. Then add some costume items and props, such as cowboy hats, vests, boots, sleeping bags, sticks (for making a campfire), and metal camping dishes. And—since every cowpoke needs a horse—add a rocking horse or spring horse, too. Yee-haa!

Rhonda Dominguez
Downs Preschool
Bishop, GA

Doin' Laundry!

To a grown-up, laundry can be a chore. However, that's not the case when little ones roll up their sleeves and do a little laundry at this center! Use two large boxes (such as oven boxes) to serve as a washer and a dryer. Then provide clean donated clothes, empty laundry detergent containers,  clothespins, and a laundry basket or two. Also set up a clothesline or drying rack little ones can reach. Then watch as students practice fine-motor skills by clipping clothespins and folding clothes, strengthen cognitive skills by sorting colors and matching socks, and reinforce opposites such as in–out, wet–dry, and light–dark!

Lisa Wethington
Carver Public Schools Preschool
Carver, MA

Dramatic Play

Preschool Performers

Do your youngsters love the spotlight? If they do, then transform your dramatic-play area into a stage where your preschool performers can shine! Use colored masking tape to mark off a stage area. Then provide a few old or toy microphones, a tape player, music cassettes, dress-up costumes, and chairs for the audience. Let the show begin!

Shelley Hoster
Jack and Jill Early Learning Center
Norcross, GA

Space Shuttle

Invite your students to blast off into the final frontier of imagination with this space shuttle! Obtain a white display board from an office supply store. Spray-paint the board black or cover it with black paper. From poster board, design a space shuttle. Cut a circular window out of the shuttle; then attach the shuttle to the board. Next, cut a circle out of the board behind the shuttle's window; then tape clear plastic or cellophane to the back of it. When a child "journeys" into space in the shuttle, ask him to look back at Earth through the window and tell you what he sees. This also makes a great photo opportunity!

Bertha Cochran
St. Matthew's Preschool
Bloomington, IL

Dramatic Play

Behind the "Sea-nes"

Under the sea? Well, not quite. To make this sea scene, copy pages 115 and116; color the patterns and cut them out. Use clear Con-Tact covering to secure the pictures of ocean life to a clear shower curtain. Then hang the curtain from the ceiling near a dramatic play area or a science center that has a sea-life focus. Add materials such as flippers and books about ocean life to the area. Get ready for some dramatic ocean-life exploration!

Karen Beary
The Children's Center
Kingston, MA

Row Your Boat

Ahoy, mateys! Make the most of your ocean theme by creating a boat for use in your dramatic play area. Cut the top or side from a large box; then cut out a few portholes. Use the leftover cardboard to make a sturdy steering wheel and an anchor. Then have little ones help you paint the boat with a bright color of tempera paint. Add some oceangoing props such as a life jacket, a tackle box, and some wooden dowels with strings attached to serve as fishing poles. Then encourage youngsters to set sail into the sea of imagination!

Jennifer Liptak
Building Blocks Of Learning
Denville, NJ

Dramatic Play

A Creative Campsite

Ahh...that crisp, cool air is calling! It's time for a camping trip—right in your classroom! Set up camp in your dramatic play area with a small tent, a sleeping bag, a lawn chair, a cooler, and some flashlights. Tuck a few books with camping themes into the cooler. Add a box full of appropriate dress-up clothing such as boots, flannel shirts, baseball caps, and gloves. Keep toasty warm with an imaginary campfire made from a circle of rocks and some crumpled red and orange cellophane. Add a frying pan and a spatula so the children can "cook" a fireside meal. And don't forget some sticks and marshmallows for roasting!

Amy MacKay
Westwoods School/Head Start Program
Bristol, CT

Hibernation Station

Help your little ones experience life underground by creating a burrow in your classroom. Set up rows of chairs to create an aisle similar to an underground tunnel. Add a table at one end of the aisle to make a burrow. Drape sheets across the chairs and table. Scatter acorns and other nuts around the room for the children to gather and take to the burrow. Be sure to include books about hibernation for children to browse through while inside the underground animal hole. Now you see me, now you don't!

Kristen Sharpe
Kristen's Corner
Mansfield, MA

Frosty Friend

Build a blizzard of sequencing and size-seriation skills with this frosty friend. To prepare, stuff three white trash bags with crumpled newspapers to resemble a small, a medium, and a large snowball. Tie a knot in each bag. Next, cut out black construction paper ovals for students to use as facial features and buttons; then attach a small piece of Sticky-Tac to the back of each oval. Place the snowballs and ovals at your center along with a supply of scarves, mittens, and winter hats (at your discretion). Invite each child to don the winter apparel. Then have her roll, stack, and pat the snowballs to form a snowman's body. Have her add the construction paper features, and the snowman is complete!

Audrey Englehardt
Meadowbrook Elementary
Moro, IL

Ice Fishing

Put a wintry twist on your dramatic-play area when you send little ones ice fishing! Bring in a small plastic wading pool and cover the top of it with an old white sheet or some white plastic. Cut a hole in the center large enough to hold a plastic bucket or gallon ice-cream tub. Toss in some magnetic fish (or fish cutouts to which you've attached paper clips). Then provide a fishing pole (a dowel or yardstick) with a magnet tied to one end and another bucket to hold the "catch." Invite youngsters at this center to catch some fish and take them to the play kitchen to fry!

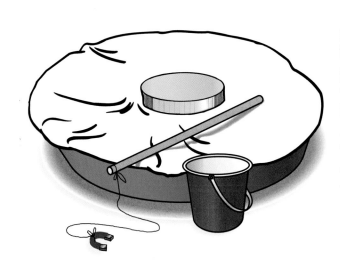

Peggy Coggins
Stewart Elementary
Cincinnati, OH

Dramatic Play

Skating at the Pond

Perk up a winter theme with a frozen pond! To make the pond, adhere white or silver Con-Tact covering to a carpeted area. Or use duct tape to tape down the edges of a large piece of polyethylene sheeting. Tape cotton batting along the edges of the pond for snow. Nearby, set up a hot chocolate stand—a small table, a pot of brown pom-poms, a ladle, foam cups, and a small container of white pom-poms will do! When it's time to skate, have youngsters remove their shoes and skate in their socks. Wheee! What fun!

Nicole Murgo
Alphabet Soup
Seekonk, MA

Going to Kindergarten

Will your preschoolers be moving on to kindergarten next year? Help them get ready with this fun transformation of your dramatic-play area! After discussing what they think kindergarten will be like, add props to your play kitchen area to make it resemble a scaled-down classroom. Hang up a calendar, an alphabet strip, and posters showing shapes and numbers. Add a small rug for a group area and set up a work table with pencils, paper, crayons, and copies of reproducible sheets. Put up a small dry-erase board or chalkboard, and make nametags for everyone to wear. Then get ready for some kindergarten commotion!

Cathy Lubold
All Saints Lutheran Preschool
Albuquerque, NM

TEC61022   TEC61022   TEC61022

TEC61022   TEC61022   TEC61022

TEC61022   TEC61022   TEC61022

TEC61022   TEC61022   TEC61022

TEC61022   TEC61022   TEC61022

TEC61022

TEC61022

TEC61022

TEC61022

Ocean Life Patterns
Use with "Behind the "Sea-nes" on page 109.

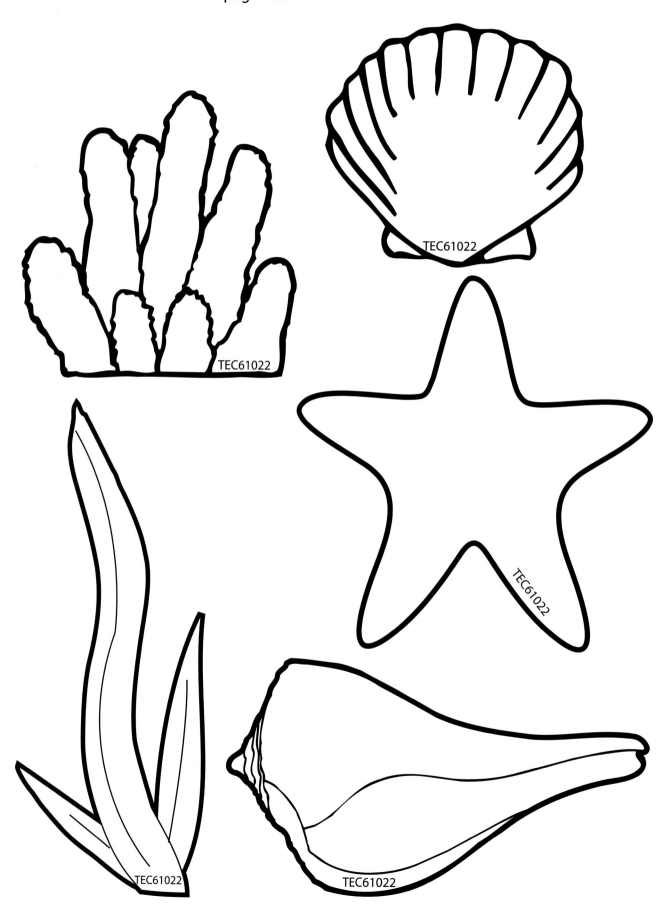

TEC61022

TEC61022

TEC61022

TEC61022

TEC61022

Rodeo Match

Set up a fun center with a western flair to help little ones practice **visual-discrimination** skills. Enlarge and cut out two construction paper copies of the patterns on page 122. Glue one set of cutouts to a file folder. Laminate the folder and the other set of cutouts for durability; then store all the pieces in a large, zippered plastic bag. Invite each youngster who visits the center to slip into a child-sized pair of cowboy boots and tie on a bandana. Have him match the cutouts to the shapes on the folder. If desired make additional cutouts so your little cowpokes can practice patterning and counting skills, too.

adapted from an idea by Susan Burbridge
Trinity Weekday Elementary School
San Antonio, TX

"Cowabunga" Cow Bowling

Your little ones will be "udderly" delighted to make and play this **bowling** game. Collect a supply of empty, clean milk or juice cartons. Seal the lids. Mix a small amount of dishwashing liquid into an amount of white paint. Invite youngsters to paint the cartons white. Then, when the paint is dry, have students paint black spots on the cartons. To bowl, a student arranges the desired number of cartons randomly or in a triangle. (If desired suggest a number of cartons based on the child's abilities.) He then rolls a soft ball toward the cartons in order to knock them down. When he has knocked down all of the cartons, he or his bowling pals "moo." This game will keep 'em "moo-ving"!

Darlene V. Martino, Palmyra Head Start, Palmyra, NY

A Place for Everything

Sharpen **categorizing** skills with this game involving household items. Gather four containers and cut out the room labels on page 123. Attach a card to each container. Next, cut out the household picture cards on page 125. Mount each picture on a labeled index card.

To play, two students place the containers and the pile of picture cards (facedown) between them. Each child takes a turn turning over a card and deciding in which room the item belongs. (Some items might be found in more than one room.) She then drops the picture card into the corresponding can. The pair continues until all the picture cards are sorted.

Holly Creep
Otterbein Day Care
Mt. Wolf, PA

Carpet-Square Puzzle

Use carpet squares to make a floor puzzle that is sure to cover **problem-solving** and **visual-discrimination** skills. Arrange four carpet squares together on the floor to make a larger square. Paint the outline of a simple shape on the large square, so that part of the shape is on each smaller square. When the paint is dry, place the squares in a games area. Encourage a child or a pair of children to arrange the squares so that the shape is revealed.

Michelle West
Denton City County Day School
Denton, TX

Farm Animal Slapjack

Bring the farmyard to your games center with this variation of the **card game** Slapjack. To prepare a game for two players, cut out the animal picture cards on page 127. Laminate the cards if desired.

To play, a pair of children sit facing each other with the cards faceup between them. The teacher names a color, characteristic, or type of animal, or makes the sound of an animal. Each partner then tries to be the first to slap the appropriate card. The first child to slap the correct animal card keeps the card. Continue the game until all the cards have been slapped. The partners then count their cards to determine a winner.

Jeri Ashford, Granite School District, Salt Lake City, UT

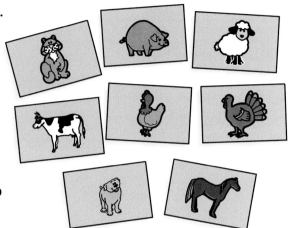

Cereal Box Concentration

Use the fronts of cereal boxes to make a **memory game** that boosts awareness of environmental print. Collect two empty boxes (regular size or individual serving) of a number of different types of cereals. (Ask parents to help with this step.) Cut off the front panels, discarding the rest of the boxes. To play a memory game, a child spreads the panels facedown on the floor. He then flips two panels. If a match is found, the student keeps the panels. If no match is found, he turns the panels facedown again. He continues until all of the panel matches have been found.

Kathleen Rollins
Children's Creative Corner
Springfield, MA

Games & Puzzles

Fishing for Friends

Help your new preschoolers get to know their classmates with this fun **matching game!** To prepare, collect two juice can lids for each child. Take a head-and-shoulders photo of each child; then get double prints made. Cut the photos to fit the juice can lids and glue them in place. Lay all the lids facedown on the floor in the center. Then provide a child or group at this center with a fishing pole made from a wooden dowel or yard-stick, a length of string, and a magnet. Have each child try to "catch" two matching lids and identify the child pictured on them. If you're fishing for a way to store this game, just stack the lids inside a potato chip canister!

Cindy Bormann
Small World Preschool
West Bend, IA

Match Me

This fun twist on the traditional game of **Memory** is personalized for your preschoolers! To make the game, take a head-and-shoulders photo of each child. Have double prints developed. Then mount each photo on a slightly larger tag-board rectangle. Laminate the resulting game cards for durability before placing them in the center. Show students how to use the cards to play a game that challenges a player to find two matching photos of each child. That's a match!

Kate Buschus
Lexington, KY

A Puzzle of...Me!

Your youngsters will love putting together these **life-sized puzzles** of themselves! To make one, unroll a length of white bulletin board paper a little longer than the child's height. Have the child lie down on the paper as you trace around her body with a marker. Then encourage her to use crayons to color in her outline and add her facial features and hair. Cut along the outline; then cut the puzzle into several pieces (depending on your students' abilities). Be sure to label each piece with the child's name. Laminate the pieces; then place them in a large zippered plastic bag labeled with the child's name. At center time, invite preschoolers to piece together these personal puzzles!

Suzanne Godfrey
FCCDC
Madison, FL

Fishing for Puzzles

Here's a clever way to renew interest in your class **puzzles.** Invite youngsters to go fishing for the pieces! To prepare, hot-glue a flat magnetic item (such as a washer) to the back of each puzzle piece. Prepare a fishing pole with a magnet at one end of the pole's string. Place the pieces of each puzzle in a separate shoebox or other container. When visiting the center, a child chooses a box of puzzle pieces, fishes for the pieces, and assembles the puzzle as he makes his catches. For variety, put the box of puzzle pieces behind a divider. Have the child lower his fishing rod so that a child seated behind the divider can attach puzzle pieces to it.

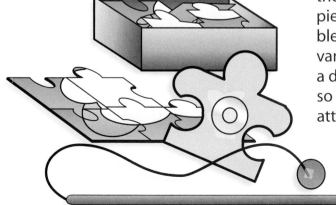

Kimberly Torretti
Greystone House Montessori
Magnolia, TX

Western Patterns
Use with "Rodeo Match" on page 117.

TEC61022

TEC61022

TEC61022

TEC61022

TEC61022

TEC61022

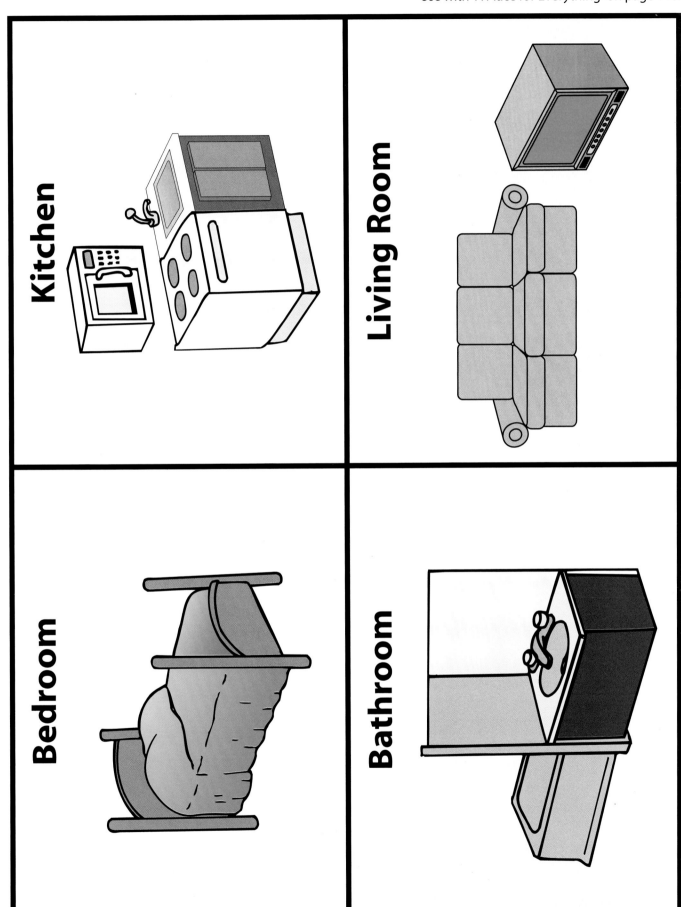

Kitchen

Living Room

Bedroom

Bathroom

TEC61022

TEC61022

TEC61022

TEC61022

TEC61022

TEC61022

TEC61022

TEC61022

TEC61022

TEC61022

TEC61022

TEC61022

TEC61022

TEC61022

TEC61022

TEC61022

TEC61022

TEC61022

TEC61022

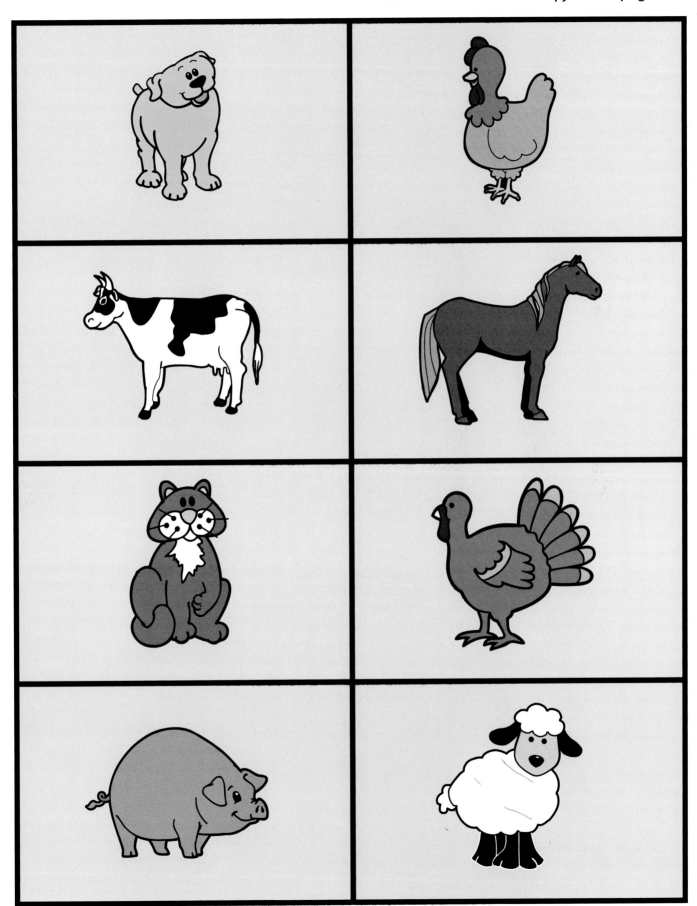

TEC61022

TEC61022

TEC61022

TEC61022

TEC61022

TEC61022

TEC61022

TEC61022